Ephesians
You've Been Adopted

Robert J. Wieland

Published by CFI Book Division
P.O. Box 159, Gordonsville,
Tennessee 38563

Ephesians

YOU'VE BEEN "ADOPTED"

Paul's "Most Precious" Letter

Verse-by-Verse

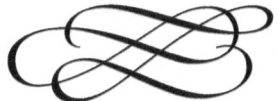

Robert J. Wieland

You've Been "Adopted"
Paul's "most precious" letter
Verse-by-Verse

Robert J. Wieland

Book and cover design by CF Industries

PRINTED IN U.S.A.

ISBN 979-8-9868765-0-4

Table of Contents

Introduction

Ephesians

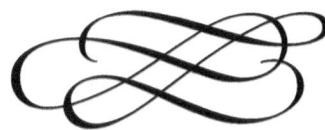

WELCOME TO A VERSE-BY-VERSE STUDY OF THE "MOST precious" good news in Paul's letter to the Ephesians. What does it say to us today? Can it still do for us what it did for those people of the first century? What was the secret of its power to change people's hearts? Why was Paul so moved to write it?

In particular we want to see how this little book in the Bible containing only six chapters, casts special light on the "most precious message"[1] of salvation by faith. Its message must yet illuminate the earth with the glory of "the truth of the gospel."[2]

If there are questions any of us may have about that message, a study of Ephesians will clear up our perplexities. The ideas that permeate the book are refreshing good news to people of all churches and religions. In fact, they are explosive in their impact even today.

---

1. *Testimonies to Ministers*, pp. 91, 92
2. Phrase from Galatians 2:4, 14

Ephesians, rightly understood, is brimful of New Testament "good news" ideas. It presents the gospel in a clear light in harmony with the work of Jesus as our High Priest in His closing work of atonement. We live in the last days of earth's history when the world's great High Priest is doing something never done in previous ages—*preparing a people to be ready for His second coming.* Our study will follow Him into His Most Holy Apartment of the heavenly sanctuary where He is accomplishing this very special work.

There are two other great letters that the apostle Paul wrote that appear on the surface to outshine this letter to the Ephesians— Romans and Galatians. Some say they're the ones that proclaim the gospel with the deepest theology. But Ephesians may top them both in its effectiveness in enlightening the world of Paul's day with these sunlit truths. Some scholars believe that Ephesians was not originally addressed to any one church, but was a general letter for all churches everywhere—for the world at large.

The reader can see for himself why this might be plausible. The letter is unusual in that it doesn't have Paul's personal notes of greetings to this or that individual, as we find in most of his other letters (which we now call "epistles"). One could conclude that this letter was intended for all the churches, yes, that it could be an "evangelism" document for non-Christian Gentiles as well as for believers. Paul wrote it while he was in prison in Rome, apparently with leisure to compose an edited evangelism message to be sent all over the world.

And for sure, if some pagan who had never heard of Christ or His gospel should have chanced across a copy of this letter now addressed to the Ephesians, his heart would have been warmed. And unless that soul had resisted the seeking grace of Christ, he would have been won to the faith. So it is quite likely that Ephesians did play a large part in the phenomenal spread of the Christian faith in that early century.

And now today, this "letter" is more up-to-date than tomorrow's media news because it pulsates with the life of Christ's urgent message He wants to go to the world. Here is that glorious gospel which "is the power of God to salvation for everyone who believes" (Rom. 1:16). It has been described as "the Alps of the New Testament."

The water of life flowing out of Paul's heart comes from a hidden spring deep in his soul. His work is incomparably greater than that of any mere theologian or philosopher. He loves people as Christ loves them! He specializes first in declaring the *objective* gospel—what Christ accomplished for the world even before we were born; then he zeroes in on the *subjective* gospel—how this objective truth of what Christ did for us motivates us subjectively to devote our lives to Him. The demarcation line between objective and subjective gospel within the letter is so sharp and clear you can't help seeing it in chapter 4, verse 1.

John M. Fowler has gathered testimonials from thoughtful readers of Ephesians:

+ The great Reformer John Calvin said it was his favorite letter;
+ William Barclay called it "the queen of epistles;"
+ Charles Dodd, "the crown of Paulinisim;"
+ E. J. Goodspeed, "a great rhapsody of the Christian salvation."

May it become to us a beloved source of saving truth in preparation for the second coming of Christ.

Paul inspired and trained other fellow-laborers in Ephesus. None were jealous of him and he never shows the slightest envy of their success. For once, in the story of his labors in Ephesus, we see a clear demonstration of what the special love of Christ known as *agape* did for a group of workers. There was Apollos, himself "mighty in the Scriptures" and "an eloquent man," but Paul worked with him smoothly and in love (Acts 18:24). There were Priscilla and Aquila who were also imbued with the same spirit that motivated Paul (vs. 26).

Apollos was from Alexandria, the second most important city in the Roman Empire. Highly educated, a Jew converted to the baptism of John the Baptist, he was an eloquent preacher. But he knew nothing of the baptism of the Holy Spirit and he needed to be instructed in the way of Jesus.

Then dear Aquila and Priscilla, in a kind and courteous way, told him what he needed to know, and thank God, Apollos listened! Sometimes we ministers may not be deficient in the same way that Apollos was, but there are also empty places in our knowledge. The Lord then sends someone to correct us and instruct us and fill in the gaps.

But we are painfully aware that sometimes our dear ministering brethren in a past era were not like Apollos: they may have been "mighty in the scriptures" and could argue, and like him had gaps in their understanding that the Lord in His great mercy sent His messengers to fill in, but they were not like Apollos; they were not ready to listen and learn. In a great degree, history has told us, they resisted and even rejected the light that God would have them accept.[3]

Now we have come collectively to the very end of time, and where "we" have corporately failed in past times we must now overcome. Time is getting short. May Ephesians finally get through to us!

There is a very important detail that can easily be overlooked. After Paul had labored in Ephesus and raised up that church and strengthened it, he left it in the care of the unprofessional elders. Were they men engrossed in the amusements and folly of that city who were only half way in love with Paul's message? Did they sneak attendance at the theaters and stadiums to watch on the sly the alluring gladiatorial combats and sports? You can be sure, *no*. These elders were consecrated men who had overcome their love of the world, and were diligent in their study of Bible truth for their day.

Elders in our churches today also have a distinct responsibility; they will earn a glorious reward by their fidelity. Paul told the elders in his day to "watch," "take heed to yourselves and to all the flock, among whom the Holy Spirit has made you overseers, to shepherd the church of God, which He purchased with His own blood" (Acts 20:31). Those words were spoken not only to ordained pastors, but to elders.

---

3. Acts 3:25; 4:1-3, 15-18; 7:51-54; 13:44-46; 18:4-6; 20:28-32

They are very important people. They "purchase to themselves a good degree" in God's estimation (1 Tim. 3:13, KJV).

Ephesians needs only to be "translated" into modern language so that the apostle is allowed to open his mind and heart to today's world, telling the content of his faith; then Ephesians again will come to life. When Paul pleads with the Corinthians, "we implore you on Christ's behalf, be reconciled to God" (2 Cor. 5:20), we know that was also the burden of his heart in writing Ephesians. Now his words are appealing beyond Corinth and Ephesus to all the people everywhere in this world.

Simply substitute modern amenities, clothing, and language, and Ephesus is transformed into a modern New York, Tokyo, or San Francisco. People are identical. There are the poor serfs or slaves who today are technically "free" but they are still caught in dreary boredom; there are the wealthy, as always, obsessed in making more money, and there are the masses in love with violence and sports. The ancient and modern worlds are virtually identical!

Ephesus had its huge amphitheater and arena, as modern cities have today. Archaeologists have unearthed the ancient theater which seated about 25,000 people bent on the same pleasures many gravitate to today. The temple of Diana was the center of idol worship in the city. Four times the size of the Acropolis in Athens, it had columns 66 feet high, as impressive to the ancients as St. Peter's Cathedral is to us today. Huge crowds attended the feasts of the goddess whose statue was believed to have descended from heaven.

Further, in presenting a challenge to the lonely evangelist of Christ, Ephesus boasted the great banking business of Asia Minor because the worship of Diana fueled the economic life of the city. Let Paul touch the economy, and will they ever hate him![4]

On the north side of the city stood the stadium where the races and gladiatorial combats were held. The people were drawn to watch

---

4. Acts 19:22-41; 20:1

men kill each other. The more violence the better the people loved it (aren't today's video games often based on a secret fascination for killing people?). The Odeum in Ephesus was another theater seating 1500 people. Self-indulgence and pleasure were all the people wanted to live for. Can you imagine—prostitution was a religious duty! How could Paul ever effectively get through with the gospel to people such as these!

But all the great cities of the Roman Empire were much the same as Ephesus. Pagan people were bored with life except for sensual pleasures of gourmet food, alcoholic drink, violence, and sex. They would feel right at home if they could be resurrected and set down in our modern cities with our sports, games, and TV amusement. As a public evangelist, Paul was challenged by these pagan people to win their attention, and then to win their hearts. He met the challenge with the message we find in his letter to the Ephesians.

Chapter 1

The Secret of Paul's Fire for the Lord

Ephesians 1:1-3

PAUL'S ZEAL FOR THE GOSPEL IS LEGENDARY. MANY martyrs have given their lives in their devotion, but no other New Testament character so poured out his soul in spectacular self-denying ministry as did Paul. What motivated him so?

Ephesians 1:1

"Paul, an apostle of Jesus Christ by the will of God,"

Through the centuries, Paul has been so poorly understood that he has inadvertently discouraged some good people. They consider his theology in Romans and Galatians so over their heads that they think he is not understandable, so why read him? Even the apostle Peter[1]

1. Peter's Greek (2 Peter 3:16) does not say "hard to be understood." Even translators have misconstrued *dusnoetos* which actually means "distorted" or "misconstrued." Peter was not scoring Paul for writing above the people's heads; he was saying that readers distort him as they read him. It's their fault, not Paul's, that they find his writings apparently "hard to be understood."

said that people in their day misconstrued Paul's letters and would "wrest" his meanings and wrongly conclude that he writes things "hard to understand." Therefore we needn't wonder that people today think the same of his writings.

Further, the intensity of Paul's devotion to the Lord, the totality of his consecration, makes people afraid. They think they could never be so all-out for Christ—they have a deep fear it may be fanaticism. They're afraid of Paul; if he goes to heaven on a first class ticket, let him have it with all the grand mansions in the New Jerusalem that he deserves. "Ordinary people" can't accomplish such all-out devotion; they're content to have a third class ticket—just so they end up somewhere inside the city. They'll be happy to sleep on the grass; they don't want a mansion like Paul will have; a shack somewhere would be fine just so long as it's inside the pearly gates. Leave us alone in our comfortable spiritual state of semi-devotion, half and half, is their attitude.

Actually, these people don't know it, but what they are content with is the "lukewarm" state that Jesus speaks of in His message "to the angel of the church of the Laodiceans." He says, "You are lukewarm [and] I will vomit you out of My mouth" (Rev. 3:15, 16; a closer rendering of the Greek would be, "You make Me so sick at My stomach, I feel like throwing up!").

This half-and-half attitude deeply disappoints Jesus, for the truth is that Paul's total devotion to Christ was the appropriate response of *any believing* person to the tremendous self-sacrifice of Christ in giving Himself for us. Paul's response was not an extreme measure of devotion; it was only a proper mirror-reflection of Christ's devotion for us. Water merely reached its own level in Paul's devotion.

But this is what many people have never been privileged to grasp. May this book be so clear that many will be privileged *to see* what Paul saw; for it was what the apostle *saw* that motivated him. He was not trying to earn a reward in heaven—the idea probably never crossed his mind.

In his second letter to the Corinthians he discusses how people felt about him, and goes into quite some detail:

1.   He wants above all else to defend his ministry before them: "We persuade men, ... and I also trust are well-known in your consciences" (5:11).

2.   He wants to give them occasion to glorify God on his account: "We do not commend ourselves, ... but give you opportunity to glory on our behalf" (vs. 12).

3.   He recognizes they may be inclined to think he is extreme or fanatical: "If we are beside ourselves, it is for God; or if we are of sound mind, it is for you" (vs. 13).

4.   But the source that stirs him to such apparently extreme devotion is the far more prodigious or extravagant love of Christ—for him and for us: "The love of Christ constrains us" (vs. 14, KJV). Paul *saw* very clearly what that love means. The idea that he has learned regarding its dimensions has captured his soul; nothing the world can offer him henceforth can compare. Paul's devotion is at the opposite spectrum from self-righteousness. Sensing himself the humblest of men, the most unworthy, still he can with no embarrassment tell people to "follow me" (Phil. 3:17; 1 Thess. 1:6).

Paul knows that the love of Christ has found an enthusiastic disciple in himself, and it is not sinful arrogance for him to say so.

5.   This inquiry into the secrets of Paul's inner heart will explain the mystery of his apostleship. "In Christ" he is sure of his calling. Transcending the vagaries of emotion that are up one day and down the next, solid logic has captured Paul's soul forever: "We judge thus: that if One died for all, then all died" (2 Cor. 5:14). Just that simple, like 2 + 2 = 4!

It's an inescapable equation: all men belong in the grave! All men *would be dead* if One had not died for them, instead of them. That puts "all men" under a common obligation, and Paul simply recognized the truth of it.

From the day of his conversion on that road to Damascus, he has reckoned that *he does not belong to himself.* He has no idea that self-sacrifice is involved on his part; he deserves no compliments or praise. What he realizes he deserves is only the grave, so everything he has that is better than a grave has to be a gift of God's grace occasioning joy and gratitude.

Here is the Paul who writes this letter "to the Ephesians." He has to share the treasure he has found "in Christ."

> 6.   So, we need to get acquainted with the author of "the letter to the Ephesians" so we can better understand why he wrote it. Before his conversion, he had fully expended his energies in fighting against God; he actually hated Jesus Christ and His followers, "breathing threats and murder against the disciples of the Lord, ... so that if he found any who were of the Way, whether men or women, he might bring them bound to Jerusalem" (Acts 9:1, 2).

Combined with this persecuting zeal was a keen intellectual grasp of the theology of apostate Judaism. At this time he *was* a wild fanatic in the utmost limits of legalism. No one can be further from the Lord than a legalist fanatic who thinks he is holy and righteous because of his legalism. A steel armor encases the heart. Paul is not just mouthing polite phrases of contrition when he says he is "chief" of sinners (1 Tim. 1:15), "one born out of due time, ... the least of the apostles, ... because I persecuted the church of God" (1 Cor. 15:9); *he tasted the depths of a hellish hatred of the Savior.* Living before the time of the remnant church, no one has ever in anticipation known more intimately the "dragon's rage with the woman [and] ... the rest of her offspring, who keep the commandments of God and have the testimony of Jesus Christ" (cf. Rev. 12:17).

In the heart of the unconverted Saul of Tarsus flared the fires of the great controversy of Satan against Christ; he was wholly devoted to Satan's side. If he had not been converted when he was, he would very likely have authored the most devilish books of anti-Christ teaching. What would have been the teachings of Saul of Tarsus worked out in the dogmas of the Great Apostasy of the Dark Ages which he described to the Thessalonians in his second letter (2:1-10)?

7.   It was divinely appropriate that this intimate cohort of Satan should be converted on that road to Damascus when he "saw a light from heaven, brighter than the sun, shining around me and those who journeyed with me. And when we all had fallen to the ground, I heard a voice speaking to me and saying in the Hebrew language, 'Saul, Saul, why are you persecuting Me? ... I am Jesus, whom you are persecuting'" (Acts 26:13-15).

Just like Jesus confronting the apostate Jews in His Father's house (the Temple) a few weeks earlier, Paul's approach to them after his conversion is totally confrontational. In a flash, all the learning of his Jewish scholarly past came into focus: Jesus of Nazareth is the Lamb of God who takes away the sin of the world! That "light ... brighter than the sun" was a vision of the cross of Christ. Every brain cell was flooded with an intensity of brilliant light; decades of distorted, perverted twisting of biblical truth suddenly were clarified. A panorama flashed like a bright video before his soul's eyes—"Christ and Him crucified."

The breath was knocked out of him; he was paralyzed until the heavenly Voice said, "Rise and stand on your feet; for I have appeared to you for this purpose, to make you a minister and a witness both of the things which you have seen and of the things which I will yet reveal to you" (vs. 16).

That vision on the road to Damascus explains his life-long obsession with the preaching of the cross. The Eleven were of course henceforth richly blessed in ministry, but a new champion who had never seen Jesus as they had seen Him came. He probably perceived Him more clearly through the word, and was now to proclaim Him to the multitudes. And thank God, Christ is proclaimed to us also in these last days as we now open the Letter to the Ephesians.

Paul's Heart-burden

Ephesians 1:1, 2

"To the saints who are in Ephesus, and faithful in Christ Jesus: grace to you and peace from God our Father, and the Lord Jesus Christ."

When one of our Popes died in 2005, some of his fans started a campaign to pressure the Vatican to make him a "saint" immediately, a process which in the Roman Catholic Church usually takes generations. Paul uses that quintessential word "saints" to describe all the people in Ephesus who were believers in Christ, joined in church fellowship. How could he?

Are we to conclude that they were perfect in their spiritual development? Obviously not; in comparison, we know that the believers in Corinth were far from spiritual maturity, so it is highly unlikely that just a few miles away in a similar Adriatic city given to idolatry, the new believers in Christ there were more mature.

Why then did Paul call them "saints"? Would he say of you that *you* are a "saint"?

The answer is yes if you have committed your heart and your life to your Savior, even if you still stumble, stagger, and fall. (Getting up again, not giving up, is the key to receiving that holy title!)

Paul addresses the people in the Corinthian church who are "called to be saints," as "sanctified in Christ Jesus" (1 Cor. 1:2), and yet his two letters to them give evidence that they were far from being perfect. But in our letter to the Ephesians Paul also makes it clear that pure unselfish living is the expected fruit of being "called to be saints."

"Fornication and all uncleanness or covetousness, let it not even be named among you, as is fitting for saints" (Eph. 5:2). Those who in the last days demonstrate such a character will be recognized as "saints" who "keep the commandments of God and the faith of Jesus" (Rev. 14:12).

"Grace to you and peace from God our Father and the Lord Jesus Christ": this is not an empty, conventional greeting like our hasty "good mornings" and "how are you's." If you had met Jesus on the sidewalk, His "good morning!" would have truly blessed your soul, because it was always sincerely genuine and caring. Paul has conveyed to you both "grace" and "peace" as coming from the Father and from Christ, not from himself—let the reader simply *believe* that they are real because the Father is real, and he will *know* these simple greetings are more genuine than any he has ever received.

Is there turmoil in your life, maybe in your home, or your place of work? As the word of God, even this simple salutation "is living and powerful, ... piercing even to the division of soul and spirit" (Heb. 4:12). To "know" that joy is Christ "Himself ... [being] our peace, who has ... broken down the middle wall of division between us, ... that he might reconcile ... both to God in one body through the cross, thereby putting to death the enmity. And He came and preached peace to you who were afar off and to those who were near" (Eph. 4:14-17). This has meaning in the most profound spiritual sense, but also in our simple, practical heart-need today. What your heart yearns for is that peace; Paul is the conduit through whom it flows into your heart from the Father and from Jesus.

Ephesians 1:3

"*Blessed be the God and Father of our Lord Jesus Christ, who has blessed us with every spiritual blessing in the heavenly places in Christ.*"

The word "blessed" simply means "happy." It is often translated so in the *Today's English Version*—in this instance as "Let us give thanks ..." To hear us say "thanks" to the Father makes Him happy also. It's a new thought to many that it is in our power to make God happy. (You end up becoming happy, too!)

Who are the "us" who are so blessed?

Of course, the believers in Christ, the "saints"! But there is a real sense in which the "us" means also the entire human race. Jesus is "the Savior of *the world*" (John 4:42), "the Savior of *all men*, especially of those who believe" (1 Tim. 4:10). Paul distinguishes between two concepts of Christ being "Savior"—one that applies to "all men," those who worship Him and those who don't; and the other that applies to believers. "All men" should "bless the Lord" because it is Christ who "gives life *to the world*," and therefore the life they already have He has given to them. Jesus said, "the bread that I shall give is My flesh, which I shall give for the life *of the world*" (John 6:33, 51). If you are a person in the world, you should therefore give thanks to the Lord!

The "life" that anyone experiences, believer or unbeliever, is the purchase of the sacrifice of Christ. In that *legal* or *corporate sense*, "all men" are "in Christ," because Christ is the second or "last Adam" who has become the new Head of the entire human race. Now when the repenting sinner believes, the legal sense becomes experiential.

As believers, those who respond to His message of love are "in Christ" *experientially*.

The good news of the gospel gets better and better as we proceed in Ephesians!

Christ has given *us* "every spiritual blessing" to make *us* happy! Paul meant that any pagans were free to read his letter, believe it, and then rejoice forever more "in Christ."

Chapter 2

What Christ Has Done for "US"

⊰⊱ *Ephesians 1:4-14* ⊰⊱

Much of this letter to the Ephesians is taken up with telling us what Christ *has* accomplished for us before we were even born. This can be described as the *objective* gospel—that is, what we had nothing to do with. It's all done outside of us.

The other portion is concerned with what *we* do, what we accomplish. It's not that in even one percent we save ourselves—God forbid the idea! But this part of the letter is concerned with what the objective gospel accomplishes *in* us. This that Christ does now in us can be described as the *subjective* gospel.

True, those two italicized words are not in the Bible; they are a modern attempt to help us visualize the two complementary gospel truths that keep coming up throughout the Bible. To mix them always produces confusion whether salvation is through faith or by works. To avoid being confused requires that we understand and appreciate the objective gospel—what Christ has already accomplished in a legal sense for the world.

In chapter one of Ephesians our apostle/author almost loses himself in his efforts to do justice to the grand dimensions of what Christ did. No language, his or ours, has words adequate to portray it. The quality of our Christian experience, our happiness in Christian living, and our fruitfulness, depend on how adequately we grasp this reality of truth. Grasp only a smattering and we are mired in spiritual frustrations. Learn to "glory" in it all, to appreciate it, then "the world has been crucified to [us] and [we] to the world" (Gal. 6:14). A thousand weary ups and downs in following Jesus become one unending triumph.

Paul is anticipating his later extravagant assessments in chapter 3 where he describes "the riches of His glory" revealed in "the width and length and depth and height [of] … the love of Christ which passes knowledge." He is confident that the Lord will yet "do exceedingly abundantly above all that we ask or think."

Before we are immersed in Paul's extensive portrayal of wonders, we must note briefly his underlying idea that lets it all come into focus. He holds this rarely seen foundation truth—the death that Christ died on His cross was the equivalent of the world's second death. Those who believe in the teaching of natural immortality of the soul are automatically deprived of clearly understanding this insight—that Christ actually *died* on that cross. Even though they pronounce the expressions about the cross, the idea of dying our second death has to elude them. Learned commentaries generally do not recognize this profound insight. But it sets free the soaring concepts that Paul wants to express.

Someone may question: "If Christ was resurrected the third day, how could His death on the cross have been the second death? There's no resurrection after that one!"

This can be understood if we recognize how "the wages of sin is death" (Rom. 6:23), not eternal life, and not a mere sleep in a weekend vacation. It was our second death that Christ "took," and He had to endure it 100% or it couldn't be true that He "died for our sins" (1 Cor.

15:3). He must "taste death for everyone" (Heb. 2:9). It is meaningless to say that He tasted our first death, for everybody dies that death (which is only a sleep, 1 Thess. 4:15-17). Scripture becomes clear when we realize that whatever death Jesus died, He "tasted" it for "all men" so that none of us need ever experience that death. But we all "taste" the first death, so that cannot be the one that Jesus "tasted" for "all men" as our Substitute.

In fact, since the world began, only one Man has ever died that second death! Everybody else has merely gone to sleep.

But someone asks, "How could Christ die our second death and not endure the physical agony of the lake of fire? Doesn't Revelation say that "the lake of fire ... is the second death"?

If we read the passage carefully (20:12-15), we will see that the lost will suffer agony far greater than the Centigrade temperature of literal fire. It's when the "books were opened" that the full stories of every man's involvement in the crucifixion and repeated re-crucifixions of Christ are laid open. Each lost person finally sees in awful detail the dimensions of his rebellion against the Lamb of God and against humanity; self-condemnation will be utterly overwhelming. It will be identical to the horror that Jesus felt when He cried out on His cross, "My God, why have You forsaken Me?" (Matt. 27:46). That horror is lethal; it *is* the death of all deaths. Those lost people will want to jump into the lake of fire as soon as possible; a total end will be welcome. When Christ was "made to be sin for us, who knew no sin" (2 Cor. 5:21), He drank to the full that bitter cup of condemnation—the kind that kills the soul (He didn't die of pain from the nails; He died of a broken heart).

Ephesians 1 is an outpouring of human gratitude for what He did for us!

Ephesians 1:4, 5

"Just as He chose us in Him before the foundation of the world, that we should be holy and without blame before Him in

*love, having predestined us to adoption as sons by Jesus Christ
to Himself, according to the good pleasure of His will,"*

"Good pleasure of His will "is a nice way of saying that this is
what God has fun doing! He loves to save lost, hopeless, ruined human
beings, young and old. If you would like to enjoy a fulfilled life, get busy
being involved with Him in doing that same work.

"Predestined" is a word that means just what it says; let's not try
to argue it away. It's simple, honest truth that God has long ago decided
to save *every* human being; He gave every one of us a page in His Book
of Life.

He has invited everyone to a place of honor at His banquet table;
the place mat with your name on it is there. His banquet is not a helter-
skelter fast-food kind of picnic. It's a seven-course dinner in highest
honor, with all the trappings extravagantly laid out. Your presence is
seriously planned. "This is good and acceptable in the sight of God our
Savior, who desires *all men* to be saved" (1 Tim. 2:3, 4).

But Jesus has had to tell the truth: many who have been invited
whose names are engraved on the invitations choose not to accept (see
Matt. 22:2-8). That's the only reason any human being will not be
saved at last!

God has never "predestined" anyone to be lost. That would
be a vicious distortion of the truth about a God of love. His divine
foreknowledge must never be confused with a supposed awful
predestination to damnation.

We used to drive on one-track roads around steep precipices in
Ruanda. The Belgians had a law that you must drive one way only during
certain hours in order to avoid collisions. If I were on a mountaintop and
saw someone breaking the law driving the wrong way at the wrong time,
I would see a collision coming. Did I "predestinate" it simply because I
couldn't help being in a position to foresee it? God can't help it that He
has infinite foreknowledge; but if He wishes He can do something we can't
do—lay that super-knowledge aside so He can love everybody with all His

heart. (Jesus loved Judas Iscariot just as much as He loved the Eleven!)

"Adoption as sons" has to be automatic for everyone who chooses to believe in Jesus because He became our Brother in the flesh when He became one of the human family. Jesus never brings any of us home to His Father's house as a temporary guest; *we're all adopted.*

And it's useless to speculate, "Can the Father love His natural Son a wee bit more than He can love us adopted ones?" He *gave* His own Son to die our second death, all for the adopted ones. It was an exact equivalence; the only "difficult" thing in being saved eternally is learning to believe how good the good news is.

It may be a thought too big for you to begin to grasp, but you must choose to grasp it or you can never be happy: the Father "chose" you individually and personally to be "holy and without blame before Him." *That's your true predestination!* It will be true forever unless you interpose a contrary, negative, rebellious will against it.

"The sinner may resist this love, may refuse to be drawn to Christ; but if he does not resist he will be drawn to Jesus, ... to the foot of the cross in repentance for his sins, which have caused the sufferings of God's dear Son."[1]

"Holy-and-without-blame" leads us to the story of the 144,000 who finally before the end of time stand "without fault before the throne of God" (Rev. 14:5). Someone objects: "That's the heresy of perfectionism!" No, *it's not.* It's simply the natural result of a heart-appreciation for the *objective* gospel being demonstrated *subjectively* in the lives of those who believe it. The fact that it's never happened yet for 6000 years in a *corporate body* of people does not mean it never will happen. A fourth angel finally comes "down from heaven, having great authority, and the earth [is to be] lightened with his glory." He cries "mightily with a loud voice, 'Babylon the great is fallen.' ... And I heard

---

1. *Steps to Christ*, p. 27.

another voice from heaven saying, 'Come out of her, My people'"
(Rev. 18:1-4).

The "mighty" part of the message is not physical decibels; it's the
power of the finally clarified truth of "the everlasting gospel," "the third
angel's message in verity." God's people will be ashamed that they didn't
"hear" that "Voice from heaven" decades, now centuries, before. It had
sounded, only to be greeted by many deaf ears.

Ephesians 1:6

*"To the praise and glory of His grace, by which He has
made us accepted in the Beloved."*

Who is the "us"? Are we lonely people, standing on the side
watching the baptism of Jesus at the Jordan River, hearing the Father
declare of Him, "This is My beloved Son, in whom I am well pleased,"
feeling that He is not "well pleased" with us?

The truth is that when the Father said this of Jesus, He was also
speaking *of us!* That word spoken of Jesus embraces humanity. God
spoke to Jesus as our Representative. With all our sins and weaknesses,
we are not cast aside as worthless. "He has made us accepted in the
Beloved"! Jesus has become the second Adam, the new Head of the
human race, and in Him we are accepted by the Father. The glory that
rested on Christ is a pledge of the love of the Father for us. It tells
us of the power of prayer,—how the human voice may reach the ear
of God and our petitions find acceptance in the courts of heaven. By
sin, earth was cut off from heaven, and alienated from its communion;
but Jesus has connected it again with the sphere of glory. His love has
encircled man, and reached the highest heaven. The light which fell
from the open portals upon the head of our Savior, will fall upon us as
we pray for help to resist temptation. The voice which spoke to Jesus
says to every believing soul, "This is My beloved Son, in whom I am
well pleased."[2]

---

2. These words have been taken from *The Desire of Ages*, p. 113.

Note how Paul continues, reiterating this good news. The "we" and the "us" embrace the human race. It's already true before you heard the news; now it becomes *real* to you as you choose to believe it.

Ephesians 1:7-12

"In Him we have redemption through His blood, the forgiveness of sins, according to the riches of His grace which He made to abound toward us in all wisdom and prudence, having made known to us the mystery of His will, according to His good pleasure which He purposed in Himself, that in the dispensation of the fullness of the times He might gather together in one all things in Christ, both which are in heaven and which are on earth—in Him, in whom also we have obtained an inheritance, being predestined according to the purpose of Him who works all things according to the counsel of His will, that we who first trusted in Christ should be to the praise of His glory."

All this is the *objective* gospel—the truth of what Christ has already accomplished for our salvation. Now he mentions the *subjective* gospel—our heart response:

Ephesians 1:13, 14

"In Him you also trusted, after you heard the word of truth, the gospel of your salvation; in whom also, having believed, you were sealed with the Holy Spirit of promise, who is the guarantee of our inheritance until the redemption of the purchased possession, to the praise of His glory."

In order to get clearly in mind what Christ has done *for* us, let's look again. If you had just bought a new luxury car, or a new dress that you really like, you'd want to look again and again at what you had just acquired. That's why we want to appreciate what is this spiritual wealth that Christ has not only *offered* us, but has *given* us if we will have it:

1.   To be "accepted in the Beloved" means to be in the family. We're not just staying for lunch; we're *in*. We have the run of the house. We can walk in past all the holy angels—*we're family*. It's beyond comprehension, but true.

2.   We have "redemption through His blood" (vs. 7). That means we have this most precious new status as the purchase of His very life—Christ *gave* Himself for us—the Son of God, the Prince of glory exchanging *His life* for us. He went to hell so we could go to heaven. Yes! That's His *eternal* life that He chose to give up. Grasp this—and the world with its glitter will never again attract you. The "blood" means worlds more than in a literal sense; "the life of the flesh is in the blood" (Lev. 17:11). Times almost without number Leviticus speaks of the earthly priest "pouring out the blood" of the victim, each time symbolizing what Isaiah 53:12 means when it says that Christ "poured out His soul unto death." That death was the real thing—eternal.

3.   "In Him we have ... the forgiveness of sins" (vs. 7). It's been *given*, "in Christ." But remember that Bible forgiveness is far more valuable than mere pardon. It means the sin is separated from us. (The Greek word for forgiveness, *aphesis*, means it's carried away. You now hate the sin, you don't want to do it again. You're free from it.)

Is it deliverance for the alcoholic, the drug addict, the fornicator, the addict of pornography? According to what the holy apostle says, the answer has to be "yes." The grace of Christ is stronger than the power of sin, because Paul says that this power is "according to the riches of His grace," which in Romans he describes as "much more abounding" (5:20). The death Jesus died must be understood here.

4.   Now there's more: the one who will receive this abundance of grace is given "wisdom and prudence" (vs. 8), or as the NEB puts it, God "has lavished on us ... insight." It's not that your IQ gets better (maybe it does!); but your discernment and understanding get better.

5.   That includes the insider-knowledge of God's hidden purpose now disclosed, which Paul again says is the Father's "good pleasure" (vs. 9), or to put it bluntly in a modern word, it's the fun that God has in this plan of salvation. He loves to watch somebody who is down and out transformed into someone reckoned equivalent in value to His own Son.

6.   The Father purposes to "gather" all things in heaven and earth in His Son—and there His redeemed people are the centerpiece of it all (vs. 10).

7.   An "inheritance" (vs. 11) is yours; wealth left to you by virtue of your relationship to Christ—it's the entire earth made new. And heaven way beyond.

Paul can't find words in Greek to tell it all, and we can't find them in English to tell it adequately! In our next chapter we will continue exploring the wealth Christ has given us.

Chapter 3

Learning the Things of God

 *Ephesians 1:15-23*

Paul's letter to the Ephesians concerns what is real and lasting in our life in this world—(a) God's acceptance of us "in Christ," and (b) what His love accomplishes for us and in us. In this light, all worldliness is vanity, for it passes away with our "perishing" outside of Christ.

We humans have a built-in obsession for idolatry; we *must* worship something or someone. This worship is just as constant as the worship of the ancient Egyptians and Canaanites for their idols. Our idols are our new cars, the limitless contents of our department stores. Our temple is our mall. The *Titanic* was once Europe's idol; look at it now.

Our human idols are our pop stars, our sports heroes, our military and political leaders. They too get old, and die.

Knowing the message of Ephesians will transfer our natural, inborn love of idolatry into the healthy life-giving worship of the one true God—our Creator and Savior. The energy that we have consumed in vain idolatry will now be directed to everlasting life which begins here and now in a new quality of life free from the slavery imposed by sinful idolatry. It will be like walking out of prison!

Ephesians 1:15, 16

"Therefore I also, after I heard of your faith in the Lord Jesus and your love for all the saints, do not cease to give thanks for you, making mention of you in my prayers:"

Again, we remember that these dear people to whom Paul is writing (whether the Ephesians or "saints" everywhere else) are not perfect people. Remember too, Paul is in prison in Rome; prisoners like to get news. Paul seizes upon the news he has received of their "faith." It's not their perfect performance that inspires him, but their heart response to the *objective* gospel of Christ; *they believe!* And that believing, that faith, has produced in their formerly worldly, pagan hearts a "love for all the saints." Transformations enough to make any pastor-evangelist happy!

Paul can't get over his joy at the news of the change they have experienced. He's always thanking God for them, and when he prays to the Father intimately, personally, all alone in his prison, he "mentions" them by name. Prayer is not a mechanical "prayer-wheel" mechanism; you don't record prayers in your computer, and then hit a key to reactivate them as in the morning you hurriedly head off for work or for school. You personally *talk with God* on a one-to-one basis and take the time to understand what He is communicating to you.

Ephesians 1:17

"That the God of our Lord Jesus Christ, the Father of glory, may give to you the spirit of wisdom and revelation in the knowledge of Him,"

There are specific items that Paul is asking for. Jesus said, "Ask, and it will be given to you" (Matt. 7:7), and Paul is taking advantage of the offer, naming what he wants the Father to give these people:

1.   The *"spirit of wisdom."* It's greater than some specific knowledge for this or that trivial situation that is of passing interest; it's a *residing* gift of perception and good judgment constantly abiding in the heart.

But it's from "revelation," not something that is original with the "saint." It's never a charged battery that can function on its own; it always has to be connected to the mains where "revelation" is constantly in process, moment by moment.

What Paul is praying the Father to give the Ephesians is that they may become active participants in the plan of God for saving the world. For the humblest believer in Jesus, that's a connection with the Father as real and vital as it has ever been for any ordained prophet. It may not be as intense, but it's real.

2.   *Paul's prayer is for us, too.* John describes the process by which in his case this "spirit of wisdom" came in steps. His principle makes sense for us: "The Revelation of Jesus Christ, which [1] God gave [2] Him to show His servants. … And He sent and signified it by [3] His angel to [4] His servant John, who [5] bore witness to the word of God, and to the testimony of Jesus Christ, and to all things that he saw" (Rev. 1:1, 2).

If you haven't been conscious of such a vital connection with God, that does not mean that it's not His plan for you, or that it isn't already becoming true in your life. Paul wrote during the first generation of Christians 2000 years ago, but there are prophetic links that bind his message to us who live in this antitypical Day of Atonement.

Wonderful people as the first century Christians were, they were not spiritually mature in readiness for the literal second coming of Jesus.

They enjoyed the High Priestly ministry of Jesus in His *first* apartment work in the heavenly sanctuary—that prepared them for death and a part in the resurrection that takes place at the second coming of Jesus. Wonderful work!

But we are living under Christ's ministry in the *second* apartment, the time of the *cleansing* of the sanctuary. His goal now is to prepare a people for His second coming, that is, for translation.

Paul's far-sighted writing may have been over the heads of his people then (which is why Peter said there are some things Paul says that were often wrested by "unstable" people, 2 Peter 3:16). Paul's writing is now coming into its own; it's not over our heads now for it makes sense for us today.

    3. Paul is praying that the Lord will give us heavenly intelligence.

Ephesians 1:18-21

    "The eyes of your understanding being enlightened; that you may know what is the hope of His calling, what are the riches of the glory of His inheritance in the saints, and what is the exceeding greatness of His power toward us who believe, according to the working of His mighty power which He worked in Christ when He raised Him from the dead and seated Him at His right hand in the heavenly places, far above all principality and power and might and dominion, and every name that is named, not only in this age but also in that which is to come."

"Understanding" has "eyes" that must be "enlightened." A key idea that pervades Paul's writings is "comprehension," seeing things, grasping truth. In chapter 3 he again prays for the Ephesians, bowing his knees "to the Father of our Lord Jesus Christ, … [that you] may be able to comprehend with all saints" the glorious dimensions of the love [*agape*] of Christ (3:14, 18). Often Jesus lamented the dullness of the Twelve to comprehend what He tried to tell them. That dullness may have been forgivable two millennia ago, but is it so for us today? On us "the ends of the ages have come"! (1 Cor. 10:11). Good works that we do can make God happy, but let's not forget that a teacher is most gratified when his pupils *comprehend* what he communicates to them!

Don't go through your life with the vague feeling that you are only another digit responding to a universal invitation like a recipient of Social Security getting something paid to a number. Paul wants you to sense to the full that the Father is calling you as an individual specially and individually. No one else can fulfill as well as you some special mission in life. That's "the hope" embedded in your "calling." When at last you meet the Lord face to face, He will give you "a white stone, and on the stone a new name written which no one knows except him who receives it" (Rev. 2:17). This will be no cold presentation ceremony like a university president handing out hundreds of diplomas at Commencement; you will have an intimate tête-à-tête with the Father and a knowing glance from Jesus. You will look into His eyes and see a recognition that tells you that He understands all about you and your life and all the mysterious things you've never been able to unravel. That "white stone" will be a little computer memory special to you!

"The exceeding greatness of His power" to us is more than triumph over cancer or over some financial crisis, great as that may be; it's the power to conquer sin in our "sinful flesh" *through the faith of Jesus.* He Himself "condemned sin" and did it in the likeness of [our] sinful flesh" (Rom. 8:3). Paul strains feeble words almost to their bursting point!

This "power" includes all that was in the power that raised up Christ from His tomb. Reverently we can say that nobody in all human history has ever been as "dead" as Jesus was dead! The reason is that He died a death unlike that which any other person has ever died—the second death, the death that is involved in the "curse of God."

You have never understood what happened on the cross unless you understand Galatians 3:13: "Christ has redeemed us from the curse of the law, having become a curse for us (for it is written, 'Cursed is everyone who hangs on a tree')." Not one human soul has as yet suffered the full weight of that "curse" except Jesus.

Paul is quoting Moses in Deuteronomy: "If a man has committed a sin worthy of death, and he is put to death, and you hang him on a tree, his body shall not remain overnight on the tree, but you shall surely bury him that day, ... for he who is hanged [on a tree] is accursed of God" (21:22, 23). This was a prophecy of Jesus and His cross. Faith has always turned every curse into a blessing (for example, the believing thief crucified with Jesus was not cursed—He died wonderfully blessed). But the people believed Moses, which is why the Jewish leaders were so determined to get Jesus onto a cross, for the moment the nails put Him there they knew He could not be the Messiah—"Moses said so!"

Now think of the power that was needed to resurrect that one Man who so fully suffered the curse of God! More power was needed to raise Him than all the power that will be exercised in resurrecting the billions in the coming "first resurrection"! *And that is the power that is given to you by which we will overcome sin in our sinful flesh!*

Ephesians 1:22, 23
"And He put all things under His feet, and gave Him to be head over all things to the church, which is His body, the fullness of Him who fills all in all."

When Jesus said that "the gates of hell shall not prevail against" His church (Matt. 16:18, KJV), He stirred up the white-hot hatred of Satan and his evil angels. They became determined that the gates of hell *shall* prevail against that church. This explains the mysterious enmity that arises against Christ's church on earth. Attacks from the outside are not as mysterious as those that arise continually from inside. Solid truths that in the past were believed wholeheartedly are now undermined in sly ways within the church.

Although "Babylon is fallen" there is a hankering to import doctrines and worship patterns from popular religion, a modern counterpart of ancient Israel's cry, "Make us a king to judge us like all the nations" (1 Sam. 8:5). Much of that apostasy was not due so much to the depravity of the believers in Israel as to the "mixed multitude" which had always been a hindrance to the work of the Holy Spirit. We must not invite the "mixed multitude" today to dictate the future of the church.

In the days of the Judges, intermarriage with the Canaanites was frequent, as is the accession today into the church of those who have never been converted to Christ. Thus the modern church, like ancient Israel, is often a "mixed multitude."

But there is good news for sincere people who are perplexed about the integrity of the organized church. Although it has often become so worldly and so irreverent in its worship practices that many feel driven to leave and they are tempted to doubt that "the gates of hell shall not prevail against" it, still the Father has given Christ "to be head over all things to the church, which is His body." His will will be done on earth, as it is in heaven (Matt. 6:10).

You must believe and claim that word of God. As Jesus walked into the polluted Temple and claimed it as "My Father's house" and expelled the polluters, overturning their tables and scattering their money all over the floor, so there is a sense in which faithful believers in Jesus must claim His headship over the church even today. But this is always by faith and not through force!

It will be a hand-to-hand, fierce battle of faith. But it must be waged by believers themselves; they must claim the church for Christ because the Father in His word has appointed Him to be its Head. There is something that those who believe in Jesus must do themselves and not wait for Jesus to do for them. The dilatory "Lamb's wife" must not wait for her Bridegroom-to-be to dress her for the wedding; no bridegroom ever has dressed his bride for the wedding! The Bride of Christ must "make *herself* ready" (Rev. 19:7, 8).

Understanding what's going on will solve the problem of non-denominational "home churches" that spring up when the true "Lamb's wife" is tempted to despair of her divinely ordained identity. If all who truly believe in Christ leave the organized church, this will be exactly what the Enemy wants to happen! Don't let it happen!

So; stay in the church. Claim it for Jesus!

What has our Lord done for us? That's our next chapter.

What Christ Has Saved Us From

Chapter

4

 Ephesians 2:1-10

AFTER NEARLY TWO MILLENNIA SINCE PAUL WROTE THIS letter to the Ephesians, there are still depths of truth in it that we all have yet to penetrate fully. In chapter two we read the exactly-right formula of salvation—we are saved "not of works" but "by grace ... *through* faith, and that not of [ourselves]; it is the gift of God" (vs. 8). When we say that we are "saved through faith" we don't want to give the impression (or have the idea) that our own exercise of faith is the cause or the means of our salvation. No one in the hereafter will boast, "Yes, the Lord saved me, but I did my part: I did the work required, I believed—that's why I'm here. I helped save myself." Utterly wholehearted thanks will pour out of our souls for all time and eternity. (To believe is not a work!)

We all long for clearer, sharper understanding of what it means to be saved, because of "the riches of [God's] grace, ... the *gift* of God." If we have been "saved ... *through* faith," we will bear fruits of "good works" which are "His workmanship, created in Christ Jesus" (vss. 9, 10). All our reading the Bible is useless if it doesn't result in "good works." Although they don't save us, they are an important evidence that we have truly believed and that our pride and arrogance have been humbled by appreciating that grace. That's included in what it means to "believe."

An important part of "good works" which are the fruit of mature faith is a preparation of heart and life for the second coming of Jesus— not just getting ready to die. Not until the second advent can God's people safely claim graduation out of our "rich-and-increased-with-goods" complex which has continued to "frustrate the grace of God" (Gal. 2:23, KJV) for centuries. We are living in this "time of the end" which began, according to Daniel (11:35; 12:4) at the end of the 1260 years of papal dominance. We will want to "walk softly" as we come to chapter two of Ephesians; this is the time to pray, as Paul told us, that "the eyes of [our] understanding" may be "enlightened." Ephesians has never been "present truth" so vital to understand as it is just now.

We are living in this "time of the end," the cosmic Day of Atonement, the hour of the *cleansing* of the sanctuary. Therefore our reading of Ephesians is prefaced by the conviction that we live in an hour of supreme crisis. *The Lord Jesus wants to return the second time.* He will forever retain His human nature so that He is still a Man seated at the right hand of His Father in heaven. All humanity is bound up there with Him. He is an eager bridegroom who wants the wedding to come. We know that the reticence of His Bride-to-be to prepare herself for "the marriage of the Lamb" has been for Him a disappointment beyond description. The great controversy between Christ and Satan has not yet been finally settled even though Christ won His victory on His cross two millennia ago; His people now have a vital part in this *final* outworking of the issues. This message of Ephesians will come into its own in this "time of the end."

Ephesians 2:1-3

"You He made alive, who were dead in trespasses and sins, in which you once walked according to the course of this world, according to the prince of the power of the air, the spirit

who now works in the sons of disobedience, among whom also
we all once conducted ourselves in the lusts of our flesh, fulfilling
the desires of the flesh and of the mind, and were by nature
children of wrath, just as the others."

"We all," says Paul; this describes our fallen nature we have "all" inherited from our fallen head, Adam. Give us enough time and if we had no Savior to save us from ourselves, we would be where any lost soul in the world is today. When you hear of something terrible someone has done, never say, "I could never do that!" You don't know what you could do if there isn't Someone who saved you—Jesus.

It was and still is the natural thing for us to do, to "walk according to the course of this world." It's the "dead" way, the way of "perishing" that John 3:16 speaks of ("that whoever believes … should not perish"). Life for those who walk after the world is a ceaseless process of perishing.

The Enemy of Christ in the "great controversy" is a "prince," a "spirit" who commands the world. His following is assured; every baby born into the world who doesn't learn of Jesus inevitably grows up to be a follower of this evil "prince" because the desires of his "flesh" and of his "mind" are naturally devoted to self. Every one needs the Savior!

Of course, no baby ever cries because some other baby is hungry; we smile because the baby is so self-centered; we watch the exhibitions of self in our little ones and we are amused, but unless the gospel principle of denying self can be introduced, this new person will become another "child of wrath," says Paul, "just as the others." The love of money is the root of all evil because its primary root is the love of self. That's the legacy of all the sons and daughters of the fallen Adam.

Can the love of Christ take precedence over this basic, inborn love of self which fulfills "the desires of the flesh"? Martin Luther said we can't stop the birds flying over our head, but we can stop them making a nest in our hair. That's a homely way of saying we need the gospel. Those "desires of the flesh" are natural, they come unbidden. Temptation arouses the lusts within; but as we read further in Ephesians we find that there is power in the love of Christ that conquers the most alluring temptations.

We "once conducted ourselves in the lusts of our flesh, fulfilling" them, says Paul; we were slaves to lust. In these last days this "prince of the power of the air," this "spirit" of "disobedience," has greatly intensified sexual temptations. Immorality has even invaded the ranks of the clergy; one great church has paid a billion dollars in efforts to settle sexual lawsuits against its clergy. A man who came to me once for counseling said he wished he could gouge out his eyes. He dreaded what he thought was the overmastering power of pornographic allurement. Even the Internet is full of the plague.

This greatly intensified appeal of temptation leaves honest-hearted, sincere people crying out, "Who will deliver me from this body of death?" (Rom. 7:24). Illicit sex has a vise-like grip on human nature. People yearn for deliverance from the horror of this captivity. To a great extent AIDS is a fruit of yielding to sensual temptations that God has lovingly forbidden us to indulge. But multitudes think it is hopeless to resist. This "prince of the power of the air" wants to destroy the human race, and he is trying to convince humanity that it's hopeless to resist him!

Now comes Paul's revelation of salvation:

Ephesians 2:4-7

"But God, who is rich in mercy, because of His great love with which He loved us, even when we were dead in trespasses, made us alive together with Christ (by grace you have been saved), and raised us up together, and made us sit together in the heavenly places in Christ Jesus, that in the ages to come He might show the exceeding riches of His grace in His kindness toward us in Christ Jesus."

John M. Fowler offers this striking comment:

> "The apostle introduces the glorious alternative available
> to this pathetic lot in two dramatic words, '*But God ...*'
> These two words may be among the Bible's most beautiful
> words. We were dead, *but God*; we were rebels, *but God*; we
> were under judgment of death, *but God*; we were aliens and
> strangers, *but God*; Satan may seem triumphant, *but God*"
> (*Study Guides to Ephesians*).

Muslims believe that Allah is "merciful," but Paul goes further
and establishes *how* God is merciful by linking His mercy to His love,
which in Paul's vocabulary is a special word, *agape*. The apostle John
reaches the zenith in portrayals of the character of God by declaring
simply yet profoundly that "God is *agape*" (1 John 4:8). *Agape* is what
is missing in Islam, indeed, it has also become missing in much of
modern professions of Christianity.

The reason is that a very popular teaching, embraced by the great
bulk of Christian people, acts as a smoke screen or as clouds that cover
the snows of Kilimanjaro; it hides *agape*. The doctrine of the natural
immortality of the human soul which is embraced by most Roman
Catholic and Protestant churches (and of course in Islam) came
originally from ancient paganism and has been imported into popular
Christianity. Multitudes are totally unaware how it happened.

At first thought it is assumed that it doesn't matter whether
or not we believe in natural immortality; we still believe in the cross
because we put it up on our church steeples and we wear it around our
necks. But we can't grasp what happened on the cross if we believe in
that natural immortality teaching. Here's why:

The Bible says that "Christ *died* for our sins" (1 Cor. 15:3), but
if natural immortality is true, He didn't! If you believe in natural
immortality, you can't believe that anybody will ever die; all go to
heaven or to hell in eternal life-consciousness. (Paul says that the first
death is a "sleep," 1 Thess. 4:16, 17.) That's why popular religion sends

people straight to heaven when they die or straight to hell (or to Rome's invention of "purgatory"). But the Bible teaches that when people die, they "sleep" and await either the first resurrection or the second—the first being "blessed and holy" and the second, "unto damnation" (Rev. 20:6; John 5:29). That expression, "Christ died …" means that He actually died the real, genuine death which is what the Bible calls "the second death" (Rev. 2:11; 20:14). That only is the real thing!

The Bible goes into great detail in describing the nature of the death that Jesus died. Isaiah says that He "poured out His soul unto death" (53:12). He "emptied Himself" (Phil. 2:7). No man has ever done that other than Christ, for no man ever had a divine soul of which to "empty Himself"! Jesus described the death he was dying when He cried out as no other man has ever cried, "My God, why have You forsaken Me!" (Matt. 27:46). No other man has ever borne the full weight of such a forsakenness, for he never had the divine consciousness to realize it.

The Bible consistently teaches that man is by nature mortal and that immortality is something *given* to man only by Christ. Thus in one stroke, the superstitious fear of an eternally burning hell in consciousness is removed; the character of God begins to shine in its natural clarity as truly being "mercy." God could never be happy in eternity with a burning hell in perpetuum filled with tortured humans. Neither could you be happy in such a heaven!

When Paul says that God "made us alive together with Christ," he means He saved us from that same second death that had claimed Christ! You have infinitely more reason to be glad that you can take your next breath if you can realize the price that Christ paid to "make you alive"!

Paul says that you and I were "dead with Christ" in order to have been "made alive … with Christ." "Alive" takes on an enormously greater meaning. You were born as all babies are born, and that birth was the beginning of your existence in this universe; but Paul perceives a deeper spiritual meaning—your birth was in fact a resurrection from what would have been for you the horror of the second death! And he can't bring himself to say it without throwing in again, "by grace you have been saved"! The Father simply sent His Son with the command, "Save that person!" And He did—you! Paul speaks of what it means to "frustrate the grace of God" (Gal. 2:21, KJV). Let that grace have its way with you; don't resist or frustrate it.

And where now is our new home? You may still have your earthly residence in a shack in Slum Town, but Ephesians is stratospheric writing. So Paul has to say that God has "made us sit together *in heavenly places* in Christ Jesus." The sitting is "together" with Him; a shack in the slums is better than being nailed to a cross, so that any living condition now short of crucifixion is something to be thankful for—difficult as that may seem to be. But seriously, the Lord Jesus has promised that He lives with you! His presence transforms your humble home into His palace.

Don't mock this holy truth, or even let yourself doubt it. His presence with us is most real; only sinful unbelief will deprive us of the joy of its comfort.

And what is His greatest "pleasure," His "fun"? Showing off the purchases of His great sacrifice throughout the wide universe, "that in the ages to come He might show [display] the exceeding riches of His grace in His kindness toward us in Christ Jesus." We can understand this just a little if we think how a father or a mother loves to show off their child; their lives are bound up with the little one—and it's only natural that God the Father loves to "dote" (that's not the best word, but what's a better one?) on His adopted children!

And all this glorious destiny, God has prepared for us long ago. Not that He has predestined anyone to be saved against his will—He can't do that to anyone; but He prepared it all "beforehand" that we should walk in all these "good works," to our eternal delight and to His eternal joy as well.

Ephesians 2:8-9

"*For by grace you have been saved through faith, and that not of yourselves; it is the gift of God, not of works, lest anyone should boast.*"

Here we have the classic, inspired formula that forever ends all controversy and confusion! Paul, thank you! No angel could have said it more plainly! You have cleared up all the controversy that has raged through the centuries about "faith and works."

It may be popular to say "we are saved by faith," but that is not the precisely accurate definition: rather, "by *grace* you have been saved." Faith is not far away: the grace operates "*through faith.*" The latter is only the appreciation of the former.

When and where was the saving grace revealed? *At the cross.*

Whose grace is it? "*For the grace of God that brings salvation has appeared to all men*" (Titus 2:11).

Is it possible for us to resist this grace? Paul says, "*I do not set aside [frustrate, KJV] the grace of God, for if righteousness comes through the law, then Christ died in vain*" (Gal. 2:21).

Does this grace of God wipe out the reality of obedience to all the commandments of God? *This grace of God "teaches us to deny ungodliness and worldly lusts, we should live soberly, righteously, and godly, in this present age*" (cf. Titus 2:12). We have teacher!

What are the dimensions of this grace? "*Where sin abounded, grace abounded much more, so that as sin reigned in death, even so might grace reign through righteousness to eternal life, through Jesus Christ our Lord*" (Rom. 5:20, 21).

Therefore, which is stronger—our wicked, sinful nature, or this much more abounding grace? *Astonishing as the answer is to many, the simple truth is clear: there is no temptation that Satan and all his evil angels can invent that is not weaker than the corresponding grace that "abounds much more."* Don't let yourself think upside down; think the pure Bible good news: it is better news than we have thought.

This means, of course, that the blessed truth of the pure Good News of Ephesians says that it is easier to be saved at last, than to be lost—if only we appreciate how that grace is revealed—in the cross of our Lord Jesus Christ.

Ephesians 2:10

"For we are His workmanship, created in Christ Jesus for good works, which God prepared beforehand that we should walk in them."

The more we read, the more obvious the truth becomes: the "good works" are not inventions of our own; God "prepared" them "beforehand." They are "prepared" in the same way that ripe, delicious peaches were "prepared beforehand" before you even planted your peach tree. In the vast creation of God, the spiritual fruit of a converted heart is grander than the Lord's most magnificent physical creations. The Greek word rendered "prepared" is *poiema*, from which we derive our word "poem." Think of a beautiful poem—how was it "created"? From someone's gifted mind, or heart.

The "good works" which are like David's poems about Christ, beautiful in conception, are not done by automatons; they are the fresh, original "creation" of a converted heart which has now been reconciled to God, and thus loves "all men" in Him. God Himself enjoys the spontaneous beauty of these "poems" of ours.

The joy of the "poet" of these "good-works-poems" is reward enough for him. He never thinks of any "crown" to be given him in the judgment day; they are the product of his own free-will. And we realize that we didn't invent any of our "good works." God "prepared beforehand that we should walk in them," and no joy could be greater than growing up in the "family of God" to realize our full maturity in Him.

Our next chapter explores the depths of meaning in the words, "the blood of Christ."

What the Father Has Done for "All Men"

 Ephesians 2:11-22

Chapter 5

HAVE YOU EVER WANTED TO STAY AWAY FROM A PARTY for fear you wouldn't be welcome? Many feel that way about going to God's "welcome party" for people who will live in His New Jerusalem. They are afraid of Him, innocently so. They would rather not even try to be saved. These people need to realize now that they are welcomed *already*.

The "welcome" is in Paul's letter to the Ephesians! It's spoken by the Lord through His word. He honors His word in the Bible. Jesus told the Jews that He said nothing of Himself, but only what the Father told Him. "I have not spoken on My own authority; but the Father who sent Me gave Me a command, what I should say and what I should speak" (John 12:49). It was through the Bible, the actual Old Testament that Jesus held in His hands, that the Father spoke to Him. All the wonderful things that Jesus said in His ministry, He garnered from His reading of that Bible!

Likewise, when you let the Father speak to you *through the Word*, you will know the welcome is yours *now* as surely as when you hear Him repeat it in that coming glad day when you see Him.

As a review, we have read in chapter one of Ephesians how the Father has already:

1.   "Blessed us [that's everybody!] with every spiritual blessing in the heavenly places." (The fact that some people refuse the "blessing" doesn't mean it hasn't been given to them.)

2.   "Predestined us to adoption as sons" (but of course we can refuse).

3.   Enjoyed His "good pleasure" in doing this—that's the "fun" He gets in His plan of redemption. (God deserves some "pleasure"!)

4.   In Christ He *has* given us "redemption through His blood"—that is, past tense. The blood was shed for everybody; therefore all *have been given* that redemption, even if many reject it.

5.   *He has* given us "the forgiveness of sins." The word means separated them from us (we can be stupid and take our sins back again! They were cast into the depths of the sea like the *Titanic* resting deep down; but people have retrieved things out of the *Titanic*).

6.   He gives us as much "wisdom and prudence" as we are willing to receive (let's not shrug it off as proud "know-it-alls").

7.   "*He has* made us accepted in the Beloved" (that's our "welcome!").

Let's not stop to question if all this is true for that could be unbelief; He has said it.

Ephesians 2:11-13

"Therefore remember that you, once Gentiles in the flesh—who are called Uncircumcision by what is called the Circumcision made in the flesh by hands—that at that time you were without Christ, being aliens from the commonwealth of Israel and strangers from the covenants of promise, having no hope and without God in the world. But now in Christ Jesus you who once were far off have been made near by the blood of Christ."

One of God's favorite words is "remember." For example, "Remember the Sabbath day, to keep it holy" (Ex. 20:8—the key to a life of endless happiness in the Lord!). Now the apostle tells us to "remember" where we came from in our "past." Isaiah tells us to remember: "Look to the rock from which you were hewn, and to the hole of the pit from which you were dug" (51:1). Rather humbling memories!

The Lord reminded the great King David of his lowly origins. He told the prophet Nathan to tell him, "Thus says the Lord of hosts, 'I took you from the sheepfold, from following the sheep, that you should be ruler over My people Israel'" (1 Chron. 17:7). If David had always remembered where he had come from, he would never have fallen.

Now, says the Lord to us in Ephesians, remember your past, what it was like before you learned of your Savior. You knew nothing but the empty, boring "perishing" existence of the pagans with their drinking, sex orgies, and wild parties that left them drunk and disheveled with their hopeless deaths. "At that time you were without Christ," says Paul. You felt like you were "outsiders" from the house of God, and you were! You knew nothing of the contrast between the New and the Old Covenants, and what was the good news in the New.

The contrast in the two can be summarized:

1. The Old Covenant began with the entrance of sin in Eden. It's the system of salvation by our own efforts, based on the love of self. It's the system of our making promises to

God, motivated by fear. All of us have been under the Old Covenant at some time. When Cain killed his brother Abel, what motivated him were Old Covenant ideas, while Abel had grasped the principles of the New. Even Abraham for a time languished spiritually under the Old Covenant before he found freedom in the New. The Old Covenant is the disciple Peter promising Jesus that he will never deny Him (but you remember how he did it only a few hours later). The New Covenant is *God's promises to us*—and our task is to believe them. The Ten Commandments become ten promises of victory over sin under the New Covenant.

2.   When Israel left Egypt and arrived at Mt. Sinai, they unwisely promised God they would do everything He asked them to do—a thoroughly Old Covenant promise (Ex. 19:7, 8). There is pride involved. God had never asked them to make such a promise. He wanted them to *choose* aright, not promise. The people demonstrated for themselves the futility of making the promise, for in just a few days they had forgotten and were kneeling down to worship a golden calf (32:1-6).

3.   The people making the Old Covenant promises at Sinai set the pattern for much of Israel's later history up and down, mostly down, until they finally rejected and crucified their Lord of glory. Murdering the Messiah is not the fruit of a people believing the *New* Covenant!

4.   Now Paul tells the Ephesians that in their pagan days they had known nothing of the joyous life there is in the New Covenant. "Now in Christ Jesus you who once were far off have been brought near by the blood of Christ."

Paul's phrase, "the blood of Christ," is a metaphor that evokes a heart realization of what it cost the Son of God to save us. His blood is His life, His soul, His very eternal existence which He "poured out," gave up, for us (Isa. 53:12). Just the thought stretches our hearts (as David prays, "You shall enlarge my heart," Psalm 119:32). While faith is more than superficial emotions which can be transitory, we cannot "survey the wondrous cross on which the Prince of glory died" without the heart being deeply moved, yes, *constrained* to commit "my all" to the One whose spilt blood we "see" with the eyes of faith.

We are a blood-bought people; by "the blood of the Lamb" we overcome (Rev. 12:11); by His blood we are "redeemed" (5:9); our filthy garments are made "white" in His blood (7:14); it "cleanses" us (1 John 1:9); by it we are "sanctified" (Heb. 13:12). That blood is "precious" (1 Peter 1:19).

That love (*agape*) revealed at the cross grips one for all time and eternity. A branch of Calvinism declares that if one is "once saved" he remains "always saved," but this is perplexing. Paul does say that "*agape* never fails" (1 Cor. 13:8), which seems to suggest that if that kind of love has once been understood and has motivated one, he can never forget it, either for time or eternity. It's not the once-saved-always-saved idea, but it's the once-knowing-never-forgetting idea. The prodigal son couldn't forget his father's love. It's possible for us to fall away and crucify Christ to ourselves "afresh" (cf. Heb. 6:6, KJV), but one who does so will be tortured forever by the memory of the precious birthright he has "despised" and "sold" (Heb. 6:4-7; 12:16, 17; Gen. 25:33, 34). Esau never later had a happy moment.

"Blood" is a sight that unnerves people; you would be devastated to see your loved one lying in its pool. The Lord Jesus Christ, rightly understood, is our "loved One," "our nearest of kin" (cf. Ruth 3:12), the closest brother, the most intimately beloved Person we shall ever know. How can we see Him die when we know that the death He is dying is what brings Him the curse of God in our behalf? He has poured out His all, until there is nothing left of Himself, and it's *our* death He is dying!

Now, says Paul, all of us once far-off people have been warmly embraced by His own heavenly Father. We are "in." We are *adopted children.* The Son of God is our Brother (Heb. 2:11).

Ephesians 2:14-16

"For He Himself [Jesus] is our peace, who has made both one, and has broken down the middle wall of division between us, having abolished in His flesh the enmity, that is, the law of commandments contained in ordinances, so as to create in Himself one new man from the two, thus making peace, and that He might reconcile them both to God in one body through the cross, thereby putting to death the enmity."

This reconciliation is far more than healing the mere trifle of Jews on the outs with Gentiles. Paul wants to face the cosmic issue. It's the chasm, the "wall," the "division," between Heaven and earth that's been "broken down" by the spiritual violence of Christ's loving sacrifice. And the great task was accomplished *"in the flesh"* of Jesus. There in that "flesh" was the battleground of the universe!

Paul is also speaking of the "division" that formerly separated Jews and Gentiles. He is happy that Christ has "created ... one new man from the two." He now loves Gentiles as he once imagined that he loved Jews. We will be surprised at the people we will learn to love when we understand Ephesians more clearly!

Paul is also speaking of the "enmity" that was aroused even in Jewish hearts by the old ceremonial "law of commandments contained in ordinances," the law that was swept away by Christ's sacrifice on His cross. These ordinances *prefigured* the sacrifice of Christ, looked forward to it, so that when the true "Lamb of God" was sacrificed it would be unbelief to continue offering lambs or observing ceremonial sabbaths.[1] "The commandments contained in ordinances" were not

---

1. The ceremonial sabbaths that came to an end with the sacrifice of Christ at the cross had nothing to do with the weekly Sabbath which was a memorial of

God's eternal moral law of Ten Commandments. But the "ordinances" were "a yoke upon the neck" (said Peter, Acts 15:10).

As the Son of God, Christ took into His human person this "enmity" of "the law of commandments contained in ordinances." The word translated "division" is our word "fragments;" and "ordinances" is our word "dogma." "Dogmatics" is the word that suggests the Old Covenant idea of stern, fear-induced demands (what multitudes mistakenly think is God's law of Ten Commandments!).

Paul is not denigrating that "law of liberty" (James 2:12) which is the expression of God's character of love (*agape*). That wonderful law stands throughout eternity. What Christ has abolished "in His flesh" is Satan's popular *distortion* of that law. "The carnal mind is enmity against God" (Rom. 8:7), which means enmity against that holy law of God. What Christ abolished in His flesh is that enmity!

Luther confessed to his father-confessor Saupitz, who had told him that in order to find peace with God he was to "love Jesus." "The problem is, I hate Him!" For the first time in his life Luther confessed something true of himself. (That confession led directly to his conversion and his blessing the world with the Reformation.) It's that alienation of heart that Christ abolished "in His flesh." Now come close to Him and the "enmity" will be abolished in your "flesh," too. That's another word for the new birth.

To many this is a new thought—this biblical idea that Jesus experienced "in His flesh" the "enmity" that sin has brought into the human race. The "flesh" that the Savior "took" upon Himself is *our* flesh, the only kind there is in this world, the real stuff. Since Adam and Eve in the Garden of Eden fell into sin, there has been no "holy

---

creation, and thus was not ceremonial or typical. They were part of the Levitical system that included the offering of blood sacrifices. As it would be a denial of our faith today to offer lambs for our sin, so it is a denial to observe the ceremonial sabbaths as being in any sense "holy." An observance of the fourth commandment includes remembering that "six days you shall labor and do all your work" (Ex. 20:9). Then seven ceremonial sabbaths are listed in Leviticus 23:4:38.

flesh" anywhere in the world—not one exception, not even the Virgin Mary. "All have sinned and fall short of the glory of God" (Rom. 3:23). The mother of Jesus could give Him no different kind of "flesh" than she herself had. So Romans says that "God [sent] His own Son in the likeness of sinful flesh, on account of sin: He condemned sin in the flesh," that is, in His own flesh which He "took" (8:3). Thus, for Him to have taken our "sinful flesh" does not mean that He was a sinner—a million times, No! He "*condemned* sin in [that] flesh"! He is the only person who has ever done so perfectly.

Thus He forever conquered sin in the one place in God's universe where sin had taken deep root. It was the grandest achievement in all eternity. Paul's message in Ephesians is that Christ has succeeded in "creating one new man, … thus making peace." Who is that "new man"? Jesus! But you and I are "in Him."

Ephesians 2:17, 18

"*And He came and preached peace to you who were afar off and to those who were near. For through Him we both have access by one Spirit to the Father.*"

The picture of this heavenly triumph is thrilling.

Christ came "preaching peace" to people nearby and people afar off, all alike, and that peace is what solemnizes our hearts. Who is preaching today? *The Son of God!* Don't ever say that you haven't heard Him preach! He preaches through the ministry of the Holy Spirit, who speaks through the Bible. The message isn't legalistic burdens, "do this!" or "do that!" *It's peace!* You and I may kneel to pray to our heavenly Father in some far-off corner like Timbuktu, but never too far away for the Holy Spirit to indite our prayer, teaching us to say, "Father!"

Now note what happens: *one* Holy Spirit works, joining our hearts worldwide into "*one* body" as we pray to our *one* Father. It's a "Father/religion," for the Son joins us *to Him*, and the Spirit glorifies both.

Ephesians 2:19-22

"*Now, therefore, you are no longer strangers and foreigners, but fellow citizens with the saints and members of the household of God, having been built on the foundation of the apostles and prophets, Jesus Christ Himself being the chief cornerstone, in whom the whole building, being joined together, grows into a holy temple in the Lord, in whom you also are being built together for a habitation of God in the Spirit.*"

Are you one of those blessed people known as "new believers?" I was once one! You feel strange: what will this new "family" be like? Did I make a mistake? What's involved in my new "membership"?

This dear man Paul is welcoming you, and telling you that you are now—careful, let's say it right!—*way above the angels* because you are now a member inside the "family," living *in* God's "house." The holy angels step aside as you pass by, for they respect you. There are two categories—"saints," which are people like you, and those mysterious "members of the household of God" who are not classed as "saints." You have a lot of new acquaintances to meet!

You'd never think of abandoning this fellowship, would you? The Enemy would love to entice you away; take care.

Further, Paul says you are a permanent addition to the "building" under construction, one of the "stones" that will endure the ages. From now on Heaven looks upon you as a fellow-stone with "the apostles and prophets." Your name is inscribed, along with theirs. Now you will know a lasting thrill as you read Isaiah or Jeremiah, or wherever you read in your Bible: you are "kin" with those characters! Being in the "family," your contacts with every Bible author and character who has overcome are more intimate than any video or movie could make them to be. Your Bible has become a new book!

And underneath you as a Foundation is that great Cornerstone, Jesus; the same "granite" that all the little stones are made of, because when He became the Head of the family He took the same flesh and blood, the same nature, that all of us have. And He has made us all to be "partakers of the divine nature."

Each "stone" is sentient, a living entity, each different than all the rest, each to be conferred with immortality at the coming of Jesus, each to revel for eternity in the peculiar and unique personality that he/she is "in Christ."

All redeemed by "the blood of Christ."

The Story of Agape (Christ's Love)

Chapter 6

Ephesians 3:1-21

E PHESIANS CHAPTER THREE HAS FOR ITS BACKGROUND thought the final events of the second coming of Christ. It is leading up to the grandest height any converted sinner can attain—to be "filled with all the fullness of God" (vs. 19). That is a preparation for meeting Jesus when He returns in the clouds of heaven.

This is the same as the heights that dominate chapter four—"till we all come ... to a *perfect* man, to the measure of the stature of the *fullness* of Christ; that we should no longer be children, ... but, speaking the truth in love, may *grow up* in all things into Him who is the head— Christ" (vss. 13-15). This is stratosphere Christian living! But there it is—it's in the Bible, it's possible, and we dare not disregard it.

It has to be and it will be. The climax of human history *must* take place. All the devils in hell can't forever delay it. The great controversy between Christ and Satan cannot run on forever; there has to be a resolvement, a final, total victory on one side or the other. Paul's letter to the Ephesians articulates the issues that make Christ's victory total:

57

1.   Christ proved that *agape*, the self-sacrificing love that went all the way when He died on His cross, is a more powerful force than all the sin that Satan can tempt mankind to get into.

2.   Adam lost his power of choice, *but for "all men" Christ has returned it*. His will is that every person be saved; but every person has the freedom to refuse if he wishes. (But it breaks God's heart when many do!)

3.   That choice to save "every man" includes that he become "holy and without blemish before Him in *agape*." Here is where the idea of the cleansing of the sanctuary, the final Day of Atonement, comes into focus. It was one day in the ancient Israelite calendar, the day which symbolized final judgment. It meant for those who participated a complete at-one-ment or reconciliation with one another *and with God*. And no one can be reconciled to God and continue living in sin—so the antitypical Day of Atonement means to "be holy and without blame before Him in *agape*."

Ephesians 3:1-5

"For this reason I, Paul, the prisoner of Jesus Christ for you Gentiles—if indeed you have heard of the dispensation of the grace of God which was given to me for you, how that by revelation He made known to me the mystery (as I wrote before in a few words, by which, when you read, you may understand my knowledge in the mystery of Christ), which in other ages was not made known to the sons of men, as it has now been revealed by the Spirit to His holy apostles and prophets:"

We need to pick up a little detail that we must not miss. All along, Paul has quietly been insisting that "all have sinned, and fall short of the glory of God" (Rom. 3:23), that is, all are "sinners of the Gentiles." He's not buying into the idea that the Jews are a righteous race in contrast with sinful Gentiles.

While he is rhapsodizing about God's "mystery" of the Gentiles becoming "fellow heirs and partakers of His promise in Christ," he is just as happy that *unbelieving Jews* can also learn to believe the gospel. He does not subscribe to the idea that Jews don't need the same thorough new birth that "Gentiles" need. That's what we *all* need, according to the way Paul is thinking. "The grace of God which was given to [Paul] for you" is the only source of salvation for any of us.

Therefore the bells are ringing for all of us. "In other ages" this glorious good news "was not made known to the sons of men, as it has now been revealed by the [Holy] Spirit to His holy apostles and prophets."[1]

That same gospel is in the Old Testament, but like seeing through cataracts on our eyes it was veiled. Now, since Jesus came, the truth stands sharp and clear. What Paul means is that the gospel has become better good news now than the prophets had ever dreamed that it could be.

Paul does not teach the popular doctrine of self-love known as the philosophy of "self-esteem." But he does teach the Christian ethic of self-respect. He sums it up like this: "I say, through the grace given to me, to everyone who is among you, not to think of himself more highly than he ought to think, but to think soberly, as God has dealt to each one a measure of faith" (Rom. 12:3). Our healthy self-respect is "in Christ."

To each human being on earth, God has "dealt" a sense of self-consciousness and confidence in what God has given him/her. If the divine Son of God gave Himself for us (Gal. 1:4), we have to be somebody very important! It all depends on that confidence—that Christ gave Himself *for you* and that He honors you as being what He bought with His sacrifice. He paid for you; He respects you.

---

1.   Interesting! Paul puts the apostles on the same level with the Old Testament prophets!

If He "gave Himself for us," then He must value us according to the price He paid. If you buy some goods in a shop, you make a decision to value those goods on an equivalent level with the price you are paying. That says how highly Christ regards you; now you are to look upon yourself in that light. This precludes arrogance and pride, for you know that you would be nothing of yourself if you did not have the Savior who bought you. But forever after, you hold your head high because you appreciate the price that was paid for you.

Ephesians 3:6, 7

"That the Gentiles should be fellow heirs, of the same body, and partakers of His promise in Christ through the gospel, of which I became a minister according to the gift of the grace of God given to me by the effective working of His power."

Now Paul shows us the sense of self-respect he has learned by understanding and believing this truth of his calling. Without any pride, he rejoices in "the gift of the grace of God given to [himself] by the effective working of [God's] power." With no hesitation he claims as an apostle that "effective working." He will waste no time worrying about whether he is where he should be in the Lord's plan. The normal human pride that so easily mars all of our service for the Lord is absent, because Paul sees himself as a lowly "prisoner of the Lord."

Paul's ability to proclaim the good news of the gospel is a gift of the grace of God. Please do not think that gift is limited to certain professional people who spend decades in literary institutions. Anyone who understands the "mystery" Paul is explaining, who appreciates how good the good news message is, can proclaim it! The Lord gives the utterance. But you must discipline your mind.

Jesus promised us that anyone who "believes" in Him will have a well of sparkling, fresh water of life springing up from his inmost soul to refresh anyone with whom he comes in contact (John 7:37-39). It may be evident when you talk with a child; it may be across the back fence to a neighbor; it may be in the questions he asks in Bible class. Life becomes a glorious adventure!

Ephesians 3:8-13

"To me, who am less than the least of all the saints, this grace was given, that I should preach among the Gentiles the unsearchable riches of Christ, and to make all people see what is the fellowship of the mystery, which from the beginning of the ages has been hidden in God who created all things through Jesus Christ; to the intent that now the manifold wisdom of God might be made known by the church to the principalities and powers in the heavenly places, according to the eternal purpose which He accomplished in Christ Jesus our Lord, in whom we have boldness and access with confidence through faith in Him. Therefore I ask that you do not lose heart at my tribulations for you, which is your glory."

Talk about "self-respect," consider this: Paul looks upon himself as "less than the least of all the saints"! However great the hyperbole, he is happy with this self-evaluation. It's no mere exaggeration; he knows that aside from a Savior, he would indeed be less than nothing. He can never forget "the hole of the pit from which [he was] dug" (Isa. 51:1). He has become a new "David" who remembers the humble "sheepfold" where the Lord found him.

He must constantly marvel that the Lord who redeemed him has given him the "grace" to preach the message. What makes his preaching a blessing to so many people is that he preaches "the unsearchable riches of Christ," and self is absent. His hearers constantly sense that there is a vast treasure of truth beyond in the reservoir of his mind and heart. It's deeper than can be fathomed. That's because the treasure is the truth of *agape*.

Something happened at the cross that is infinite in scope yet finite in its comprehension by the people. They each feel that Paul is preaching to them individually, yet to listen to him is to sense glorious truth just out of reach. They want to come back time and again to hear him. They can feel their souls stretching bigger under his pulpit ministry of grace. All this has to be because the preacher draws from a well where grace abounds much more than all our sin.

Paul takes men's ears and turns them into eyes so they can *see* what is this divine-human fellowship. Something thrilling is happening before their eyes—the unfolding of what's been bound since "the beginning of the ages." When you get up early and come to hear Paul preach, you are participants in a new creation. It's exciting; you can't stay home; teenagers, you know you've got to be there. You *can't* sleep late Sabbath morning! You don't want to miss a single sermon of Paul's. Any Sabbath you may witness the living creation of a new "epistle" like Ephesians!

The church suddenly ceases to be that stodgy place where all is boring, and now it becomes a kind of interplanetary rocket where it carries news that other worlds want to hear—"the wisdom of God" hidden for ages from both the world and the universe, wisdom now revealed in the gospel of Christ. The "messenger" is the church. Unfallen worlds will sit in stunned silence to hear what the church, for which the Son of God gave His blood, will have to say. And you are a part of it!

That being so, why do the people who happen to live next door to the church here on earth now seem to care so little? One reason is that the church has forgotten about her ministry to the universe, and has become engrossed in getting bigger numbers on the rolls here.

Paul is thinking of a great ministry for the church. But can the church speak to these "principalities and powers in the *heavenly* places"? Or is this a ministry that must await life beyond the first resurrection when we fondly anticipate how the redeemed will fly from world to world on vacation trips? No, Paul answers the question and says it's "now."

Therefore in Christ we *now* have "boldness and access with confidence through faith in Him." Remember, God's people "in Christ" are now higher than the angels! They are "members" of the "household." They walk in past all the holy angels who are mere "servants," into the presence of the Father, "in Christ."

So don't worry about me, says Paul. I'm nobody, like I said; but I'm suffering all this Roman imprisonment and these trials, "for you."

It gives him a little deeper sense of "fellowship with Christ in His sufferings." That leaves a smile in his heart.

Ephesians 3:14-19

"For this reason I bow my knees to the Father of our Lord Jesus Christ, from whom the whole family in heaven and earth is named, that He would grant you, according to the riches of His glory, to be strengthened with might through His Spirit in the inner man, that Christ may dwell in your hearts through faith; that you, being rooted and grounded in love [agape], may be able to comprehend with all the saints what is the width and length and depth and height—to know the love [agape] of Christ which passes knowledge; that you may be filled with all the fullness of God."

1. We learn the right way to pray—*on our knees.*
2. We learn the right One to whom we should pray—to *the Father* of our Lord Jesus Christ. The Bible doesn't give us examples of praying to the Holy Spirit. It tells us to "pray *in* the Holy Spirit" (Jude 20), but the Bible is insistent on directing our prayers *to the Father.* Our Savior taught us how to pray, "Our Father ..." Children should be taught to come *to the Father* in Jesus' name; He loves them just as much as Jesus does! They shouldn't be left to fear the Father as being far away, or too distant to care about children. Some children have a negative image of "father-ness," and they need special help. Here's where the gospel is so needed to be understood.

3. We are reminded that the church is one "family in heaven and earth." We would never want to forget or neglect our family ties. When you are baptized, you join the church which is the "body of Christ." But the church is bigger than we could imagine! It includes heavenly beings.

4. Our "inner man," our spiritual life, needs to be "strengthened." The first step is to thank God for Paul's prayer for you; His prayer is on record at the throne of God and will be answered for you if you *want* it to be. Ephesians is not playing with words; these are serious thoughts.

5. The pantheistic idea that Christ is present in "every person" is seen to be falsehood, but Christ does dwell in human hearts *by faith*. Faith is real, but it is more than raising one's hand in a meeting. It is welcoming the Lord into the heart, but again it is more than a formal word; it is letting the mind concentrate on Him like you concentrate on thinking about someone whom you deeply love.

Someone wisely said it is letting the mind follow Jesus in imagination as you read the stories of Jesus in the four Gospels. Every worldly spectacle or sound is laid aside; you give Him attention (you have to, to be courteous!). If you are learning a new language, the first lesson is very simple; be patient as you listen. Now read the Word and ponder. Be careful—there is no electronic transfer of "Christ" into your soul like moving a picture or a document from one computer to another. Watching a video or a movie is not "Christ dwelling in your hearts through faith." God has said that the Holy Spirit speaks through *His word*; nothing can supplant the Bible.

6. You become "rooted and grounded in *agape*," like a giant oak that sends its roots down deep so when the storm rages, it stands.

7. What Paul is praying for is not that you will give more offerings, or pay more tithe, or even go on more "missionary" journeys. He is not praying for you to do more "works." He

is praying that you *"comprehend"* something; *see* something; *realize* something. See what? The grand dimensions, wide as eternity, dimensions of the love known as *agape*.

8. When truly in a mature way you see and comprehend it, then you are ready for the second coming of Jesus for you are "filled with all the fullness of God." Theologians call this "eschatology," the teaching of last events. Ephesians belongs in the category of Daniel and Revelation but fills in the needed truth of justification by faith.

In our next chapter we must take time out and ponder the differences between "love" as we know it, and *agape*. The contrast is striking.

Ephesians 3:20, 21

"Now to Him who is able to do exceeding abundantly above all that we ask or think, according to the power that works in us, to Him be glory in the church by Christ Jesus throughout all ages, world without end. Amen."

Paul is not saying that the sinful world as we know it will never come to an end; the Bible is too clear in telling us that we are living in the last days, and "the night is far spent, the day is at hand" (Rom. 13:12). The "world without end" will be the "new earth in which righteousness dwells" (2 Peter 3:13).

God delights in telling us that He wants to do much more for us than we have the courage and faith to ask for. Still thinking of the cosmic struggle of the great controversy between Christ and Satan that has engrossed his mind, Paul seems willing to end his letter here with committing the church to God.

But he asks that God will empower his readers so that the church may help conclude the universe-wide struggle by bringing glory to God. The answer to his prayer is in your and my hands—in our willingness to cooperate with Him.

What Love (Agape) Does in a Believing Heart

Chapter 7

 *Ephesians 4:1-16*

BEFORE WE GO FURTHER WE NEED TO SEE WHY PAUL WAS so engrossed with the idea of *agape*. There is in it a "width and length and depth and height ... that [we] may be filled with all the fullness of God" (Eph. 3:18, 19). That would be nothing short of a preparation for translation at the second coming of Jesus! Ephesians is side-by-side "present truth" with Revelation.

Agape was the apostles' one word that encapsulated the idea of the gospel. John said that "God is *agape*" (1 John 4:8). That word in their hearts "turned the world upside down" in the time of the apostles (cf. Acts 17:6). A Greek word, it meant little until the event of the cross of Christ imbued into it meaning that had never been known before, and distinguished it from the other words the Greeks had for "love." There was a mysterious explosive in this spiritual bomb undreamed of by the world's then-philosophers.

What shocked the world was the sudden realization that what they had been calling "love" was in reality veneered selfishness. The human psyche was stripped naked by this revelation. If you welcomed the new idea, you became clothed with *agape* yourself; if you rejected it, you became its bitter opponent and persecutor. There was nothing the Enemy of Christ hated more than the proclamation of this truth. When the young church was established, the infiltration of ideas from paganism attacked *agape* and brought about the great "falling away" from the gospel that has characterized history the last two millennia (cf. 2 Thess. 2:3-7). They lost their "first *agape*" (Rev. 2:1-4).

Here are a few of the contrasts between *agape* and the popular idea of love:

1.   Our human love depends for its existence on the beauty or goodness of its object.
In contrast, *agape* loves bad people, even our enemies.

2.   Our human love rests on a sense of need, an emptiness within that longs to be filled.
Agape knows no need, loves out of its infinite wealth. God doesn't love us because He needs us or is empty without us; He just loves us.

3.   Our human love depends on the value of its object. We can be nicer to the mayor than we are to the garbage man.
Agape doesn't depend on the value of is object, *it creates value in its object.*

4.   Our human love believes it must go in search of God. Every pagan religion is built on this premise, and many Christians have the same idea.
Agape is the opposite: it is God searching for lost man. There is no parable in the Bible of a lost sheep that must search for its shepherd, but there is one of a Good Shepherd searching for His lost sheep.

5.   Our human love is always seeking to climb higher.
Agape dares to step down lower. In Philippians 2:5-8 Jesus takes seven steps in condescension until He could go no lower—"even the death of the cross."

6.   In summary, human love is based on egocentric concern—a fear of hell or a hope for reward in heaven. It

cannot discern or appreciate the love revealed on Christ's cross.

Agape "casts out fear" (1 John 4:18). It is willing to relinquish its reward. *It dares to die our second death.* Hell holds no fear for one whose heart is filled with *agape*. Jesus is its one great Example. "God is *agape*."

7. The cross of Christ is its only *adequate* revelation.
This alone can explain Paul's presentations of *agape* in Ephesians. It's an idea that will turn the world upside down again.

Ephesians 4:1-3
"I, therefore, the prisoner of the Lord, beseech you to have a walk worthy of the calling with which you were called, with all lowliness and gentleness, with longsuffering, bearing with one another in love [agape], endeavoring to keep the unity of the Spirit in the bond of peace."

This is the point where Paul's presentation of the *objective* gospel in these first three chapters of the book changes to the *subjective*. From here on he is encouraging the people not only to believe the gospel intellectually, but he is teaching them how to *live it* in their daily lives.

But even so, constantly he is saying beneath the surface that it's their understanding and faith in that *objective* truth of what happened on Christ's cross, before they were born, that motivates them to practical godliness. He will never get away from that basic premise of Christian living: "the *agape* of Christ constrains us."

"A walk worthy of [our] calling" is simply a heart-response to the love that "constrains" us. The "calling" imbues us with that healthy sense of self-respect (not proud self-esteem!) that enables us to hold our heads high as appointed "ambassadors for Christ as though God were pleading through us: we implore you on Christ's behalf, be reconciled to God" (2 Cor. 5:20). The ambassadors from a great nation believe they are living for an honorable purpose; they are important. How infinitely more so are we who are called of God for an eternal ministry.

No matter who it is that the Lord sends you to, a child in the home, a neighbor, a fellow-worker at the office or at the shop, or a student at school, *you* are the King's ambassador! You feel unworthy? Amen! That's good. Remember that, and then the Lord can use you. If you ever feel proud and self-sufficient, He can't use you. (Satan uses proud people!)

"Lowliness and gentleness" are rare character traits, even in some church work. But the ministry of the humble ones is far-reaching and lasting. These are Christlike character traits, and therefore we must expect that Satan opposes those who have them and will even persecute them. But those who are close to Christ will constantly strive to bring people into harmony with each other.

Ephesians 4:4-6

"There is one body and one Spirit, just as you were called in one hope of your calling; one Lord, one faith, one baptism; one God and Father of all, who is above all, and through all, and in you all."

Out of the welter of confusion which is modern organized religion, is it possible that there is somewhere one *true* church? Revelation pinpoints such a people as a symbolic "woman clothed with the sun, … and on her head a garland of twelve stars," who in the end of time is designated as a remnant (KJV) of "her offspring, who keep the commandments of God and have the testimony of Jesus" (12:1, 17). They are obviously the same as that "one body" of "one faith, one baptism." Since there is one Holy Spirit, it follows that His leading will produce a church that is united, a refuge from the turmoil and confusion that fills the world. There is something miraculous about the very existence of a worldwide church that is truly united as one.

The worldwide unity of this "body" is not produced by force of any kind, but by a common heart conviction of truth held by people of all languages and cultures. The true church is one because God's truth is one. Bible teaching is clear; one of the greatest evidences of the inspiration of the Bible is its harmony in its 66 books and 40 writers, writing hundreds of years apart yet in perfect unity. Now the church which the Bible raises up is likewise united as one.

Take "baptism," for example. Various congregations differ in how they understand it; but since Ephesians says "there is *one ... baptism*" should we not be encouraged to study together to find what that *one* method is and what it means?

So with all the doctrines taught by any church; they are all subject to be corrected by Bible teaching.

Ephesians 4:7-10

"But to each one of us grace was given according to the measure of Christ's gift. Therefore He says: 'When He ascended on high, He led captivity captive, and gave gifts to men' [Psalm 68:18]. (Now this, 'He ascended'—what does it mean but that He also first descended into the lower parts of the earth? He who descended is also the One who ascended far above all the heavens, that He might fill all things.)"

The message of Ephesians is constantly recurring good news:

1.   Each of us has been given a special gift of grace. We say of someone who is an acclaimed musician or artist, "he is gifted." So are you. There is something you are equipped to do that no one else is your equal, in that exact respect. Instead of wasting valuable resources of time and energy bemoaning your supposed ineptitudes, expend some energy thanking God for the abilities He has given you.

2.   "The measure of Christ's gift" is rendered in *Today's English Version* as "a particular share in the bounty of Christ." We could say that from out of the generosity of

Christ, each of us is given his own "gift." However small you may think your "gift" may be, don't forget you can cultivate it to make it grow.

3.   To support his point, Paul quotes Psalm 68:18 which describes Christ's ascension to heaven after His resurrection. It was a cosmic triumph. The "captivity" which He led "captive" was the host of saints resurrected with Him (cf. Matt. 27:52, 53). The idea is that He climbed the heights of heaven and captured the enemy's booty, and handed it all out in "gifts" to us all. He took a little band of Galilean peasants and made them the down payment on a multitude of people who through the ages since have been the "gifted" leaders of His church. Having risen from the tomb, Christ has seized the universe and redistributed its wealth! There is nothing about His coming as King of kings and Lord of lords that is modest.

4.   Paul seizes the opportunity to emphasize how Christ *"descended"* to the lowest point in the universe—the point of the second death of all the inhabitants of this planet (cf. Heb. 2:9), a willing surrender of Himself to die that death from which no resurrection could ever be hoped for. "Christ *died* for our sins," says Paul (1 Cor. 15:3)! It takes your breath away ... forever, as it were. *That* is love (*agape*), says Paul! How can you ever hold back an ounce of devotion from Him?

Ephesians 4:11-16

"And He Himself gave some to be apostles, some prophets, some evangelists, and some pastors and teachers, for the equipping of the saints, for the work of ministry, for the edifying of the body of Christ, till we all come to the unity of the faith and the knowledge of the Son of God, to a perfect man, to the measure of the stature of the fullness of Christ;

that we should no longer be children, tossed to and fro and carried about with every wind of doctrine, by the trickery of men, in the cunning craftiness by which they lie in wait to deceive, but, speaking the truth in love [agape], may grow up in all things unto Him who is the head—Christ—from whom the whole body, joined and knit together by what every joint supplies, according to the effective working by which every part does its share, causes growth of the body for the edifying of itself in love [agape]."

Whatever gift anyone has received from the Giver of gifts, it builds up the church. When you're perplexed about whether a message you hear or read comes from God or is a counterfeit from the Enemy, just watch and see: does it *build up* the church?

It is commonly said that theological harmony is impossible in the church until after the second coming of Christ. Theologians just *must* squabble, we think; teachers *must* disagree; pastors *must* preach against each other; you're not smart unless you demonstrate where you differ with everyone else. Paul says no; this "one Lord, one faith, one baptism, one Spirit" means what it says. We are to "grow up" out of our pitiful childishness into "the unity of the faith." Christ is not divided.

That means a development of character that brings God's people unto the enormously high standard of the Son of God Himself—"a perfect man, ... the measure of the stature of the fullness of Christ."

Someone may ask, "Is that the heresy of perfectionism?" No. "Perfectionism" is indeed a heresy, but this is not it; the heresy part is the idea of *perfection of the flesh.* The flesh never becomes perfect until Jesus comes. But this is Christlike *perfection of character.* The Bible does not even claim perfection of Christ's flesh. As a Carpenter, He was a careful workman, and faithful; but must we say that He never bent a nail or hit His thumb? Hebrews says He learned "perfection" by the "things which He suffered" (5:8, 9).

But let us beware of ridiculing the idea of overcoming sin, because it's what Christ died to accomplish in His people! It's the final fruit of His work as High Priest in the second apartment of His heavenly sanctuary, the time of its ultimate cleansing on this antitypical Day of Atonement. It's His work going forward just now. It's His ministry of the "growing up" of His people that they may no longer be immature, "tossed about" by confusion, but may "grow up" before His coming.

What will be their goal in "growing up"? "The measure of the stature of the fullness of Christ."

An impossible goal? It's not *their* "work" to achieve it; their "work" is to "*let* this mind be in [them] which was also in Christ Jesus" (Phil. 2:5). The "let" suggests that the Holy Spirit will impart to them that "mind" if they do not resist Him.

"Is it a sin to be deceived?" The closer we come to the close of human probation, the more tragic it will be to *let* ourselves be deceived by the clever Enemy of truth. It's too late in the day for that! It's true, there are people in the church who are "tricksters," as Paul says, waiting for a chance to deceive anyone with their supposed "new light." How can you avoid ever becoming a victim? "Speak the truth in *agape*," listen to it in *agape*, then you'll "grow up" out of the childishness that is always grasping every sensational story and idea.

"Growing up" is always painful in some ways. We once had a couple in our church who had a 20-year-old son who had the mind of a 3-year old. What a burden for the parents! What does the Lord Jesus think of a church composed of retarded-growth saints? How painful for Him!

But retarded-growth people often appear very cheerful, full of smiles and laughter, for they do not realize their condition. To those who are spiritually "retarded," Jesus says, "Thou knowest not" (Rev. 3:17, KJV). Blissful ignorance, "knowing not," is an embarrassment for the Lord this near the end of time; it's the shameful boast of His unperceptive people, "I am rich, have become wealthy, and have need of nothing" (Rev. 3:17).

The best good news comes now: the growing up process *is going on!* "The whole body," the church, is like a human body that grows in perfect symmetry and unity. It has joints and muscles and nerves and organs, and they all function in an impressive unity like a healthy human body. Paul's idea is that the truest "church growth" is not where specialist gurus come in to cause it, but where the members themselves, filled with *agape*, are adding new people, and helping those already in the church to grow.

That is the ultimate "evangelism," which will be demonstrated perfectly when that "other angel coming down from heaven, having great authority" illuminates the earth "with his glory," calling every honest-hearted soul to "come out of Babylon" (Rev. 18:1-4). And, praise God! His people still scattered in "Babylon" will heed the Voice and come!

That "other angel" is again a symbol of *a people* who have the message and are the messengers. The outpouring of the Holy Spirit as "the latter rain" will supply the holy energy. The beginning of that final "gift" was given long ago, but by many it was not welcomed at the time. But God will not permit His seed to return unto Him void; He is watching over that "most precious message," and in His providence it will bear its fruit.

Chapter

8

From Now On—Living "In Heavenly Places"

⊰⟐⟐⊱ *Ephesians 4:17-32* ⊰⟐⟐⊱

IT'S IN CHAPTER ONE THAT PAUL TOLD US THAT GOD "has blessed us with every spiritual blessing in the heavenly places in Christ" (vs. 3). We walk the paths of earth, but we live in the atmosphere of heaven. Christ was resurrected to His divine life that He had laid down voluntarily; but that resurrected life was not merely His—it's ours as well "in Him." That's how we live "in the heavenly places." Now we come to the nuts and bolts needed to put together the kind of daily living that our heart cries out for.

In contrast to the thrilling recitals of what the Lord Jesus *has* done for us, and what He *is* doing for us as our great High Priest, Paul now starts telling us how *we* are to live as converted believers in Christ. He is not "laying down the law" as a legalist; he is reminding us of the kind of fruit that genuine faith in Christ always bears. The problem is that we sometimes forget.

This converted life is never a program of works-righteousness, although you may have been confused by some devout people who invent synthetic, legalistic imitations of the real thing. Holy, happy, converted "practical-godliness-living" is always by faith alone—that is, not faith *and* works, but faith *which* works. (The "works" is a verb and not a noun.) The devil can't stop one who believes from doing them.

It's not a new schedule superimposed upon your conversion to Christ, like "fine print" not seen at the beginning of a sales contract. As the Holy Spirit originally motivated your heart to surrender your all to your Savior, so let Him continue to motivate that same surrender moment by moment, day by day. You never have to make tomorrow's battles of faith your struggle today. "As your days, so shall your strength be" (Deut. 33:25). Don't think that having gotten you started in a new life, the Lord Jesus backs off and leaves you to "fly on your own once you get up to speed." He is more concerned for your victory of faith than you are yourself.

There is no checklist where you tick off "works" item by item which you think you have performed. That can lead to spiritual pride, or equally, to despair, because it's the essence of Old Covenant living. It's deceptive because it appears on the surface to produce results— outward "obedience to the law."

But New Covenant living is a constant choice to believe the Lord's promises. It's a constant renewal of the distraught father's prayer who prayed because of his demon-tormented son, "Lord, I believe; *help my unbelief!*" (Mark 9:24). You can never perish while you pray that prayer! Even if you live to be 100, you'll still be praying it, but you'll be having victories constantly.

Paul says we are not to climb up to heaven to get righteousness, but the Lord Jesus *descended* from heaven to give it to us: "The righteousness of faith speaks in this way, 'Do not say in your heart, "Who will ascend into heaven?"' (that is, to bring Christ down from above), ... but what does it say? 'The word is near you, even in your mouth and in your heart' (that is, the word of faith which we preach)" (Rom. 10:6-8). Instead of waiting for you to *climb up* into Heaven, the Holy Spirit is *coming down* to where you are. The Good Shepherd looks for and finds His lost sheep.

New Covenant living is the kind of life that Abraham lived. We don't read that he ever made any promises to God, but he chose to believe God's promises to him.

They were these:

1. "I will make of you a great nation." In other words, you will have fulfillment,—super. You will be *somebody* (all this is Genesis 12:2, 3).

2. "I will bless you," which means simply, make you happy,

3. "And make your name great." You'll become all you really want to become, in Him.

4. You shall *be* a blessing" everywhere you go. In other words, you'll always be making other people happy. It's life to the full!

5. "I will bless those who bless you." God will reward people who help you.

6. "I will curse him who curses you." This has to be, as part of the blessing on you. You are under the Lord's special protection.

7. "In you all the families of the earth shall be blessed." That's Christ, of course; but you are "in Christ" now, so you share in that joy.

Responding to these promises is beyond the level of mere emotion; all true obedience is based on the principle of simply believing these promises, that they are made to you. You ask the Lord to hold you by the hand as you follow Him step by step; He does!

Ephesians 4:17-19
"This I say, therefore, and testify in the Lord, that you should no longer walk as the rest of the Gentiles walk, in the

*futility of their mind, having their understanding darkened,
being alienated from the life of God, because of the ignorance
that is in them, because of the hardening of their heart; who,
being past feeling, have given themselves over to licentiousness,
to work all uncleanness with greediness."*

Paul is asking these people to be thoughtful and *choose* by the
grace of the Lord to cooperate with Him. A very wise person has
written, "The knowledge of your broken promises and forfeited pledges
weakens your confidence in your own sincerity, and causes you to feel
that God cannot accept you; but you need not despair. *What you need
to understand is the true force of the will.* This is the governing power
in the nature of man, the power of decision, or of choice. Everything
depends on the right action of the will. The power of *choice* God has
given to men; it is theirs to exercise. You cannot change your heart,
you cannot of yourself give to God its affections; but you can *choose* to
serve Him."[1]

There is no limit to the number of times you can choose aright!
If some temptation comes at you often, make the choice a thousand
times a day to say "No!" Jesus did; that's how He "condemned sin in the
flesh" (Rom. 8:3, 4).

What happens to someone who is "alienated from the life of
God"? The resultant "ignorance" produces naturally that "hardening of
their heart." It happens all the time, as it did long ago in Paul's day.
Those Gentiles went to the games in the amphitheaters to watch men
kill each other, and they enjoyed watching Christians, men and women,
thrown to the lions. The people loved the excitement and the flirting
with death, so they would watch it. Human hearts today become so
hard that they can someday watch Christ being crucified and laugh.
Sexual sensuality goes with the love of violence, and becomes a driving
obsession.

---

1.   *Steps to Christ*, p. 47, emphasis added.

Ephesians 4:20-24

"*But you have not so learned Christ, if indeed you have heard Him and have been taught by Him, as the truth is in Jesus: that you put off, concerning your former conduct, the old man which grows corrupt according to the deceitful lusts, and be renewed in the spirit of your mind, and that you put on the new man which was created according to God, in righteousness and holiness.*"

Thank God, here comes that wonderful word, "But …" God so loved the world that He sent His Son into this cesspool of iniquity. We "learned Christ" like we learn a new language. It is He Himself who has been teaching us. Like a tree shedding leaves in autumn, we drop these worldly ways one by one as the Holy Spirit convicts us of this and that. Hearts as hard as granite are "renewed" and become human again. The very mind has a new life; you stop and think a moment and you realize, *you are a new creation!* You discover that "true holiness" is the only way to live a happy life. You repent that you so often shied away from it, and resisted it.

Let's count up what Paul is asking these people to remember:

1. *Stop* walking like the other Gentiles do. You have a new heart now.

2. *Put off* your former conduct, like you put off a worn-out, shabby, last year's coat. Just *put it off!* Don't pull it out of the garbage can again.

3. "*Be renewed* in the spirit of your mind." In other words, stop resisting the Holy Spirit as He renews your mind. Constantly He is trying to give you "the mind of Christ" (Phil. 2:5).

4. "*Put on the new man* which was created according to God, in righteousness and true holiness." Put off your old, put on the new. Putting on the new is easy once you

have put off the old; that's the only struggle you have. Once you see how "the world" crucifies Christ afresh, you can't be enticed any longer to follow its ways.

Jesus tells us that He is sending the Holy Spirit to us each one, individually and personally. The Lord has untold billions of people (and angels) to care about, but no matter, He attends to you as if you were the only one He has on earth. He is infinite; but because He is, He can attend to the finite, which is you.

Ephesians 4:25-28

"Therefore, putting away lying, each one speak truth with his neighbor, for we are members of one another. 'Be angry, and do not sin' [Psalm 4:4]: do not let the sun go down on your wrath, nor give place to the devil. Let him who stole steal no longer, but rather let him labor, working with his hands what is good, that he may have something to give him who has need."

After nearly 2000 years, you would think that we shouldn't need this down-to-earth, practical instruction! But we do. Jesus was the very soul of sincerity; when He would meet you on the sidewalk and say "Good morning," He meant it, and you knew it. When He asked, "How are you?" He really cared. (Often we never wait to learn how our person is whom we have asked.) Verse 25 is just simple Christlike love across the back fence. Love which is alive sees Christ by faith in each other person.

The Bible doesn't say it's a sin always to be angry. A person who can't get angry is probably spineless. But the anger is always under strict control of love, which is why you never want a day to pass without making a particular wrong right as far as possible. Satan constantly tries to intrude but you never give him permission, and he *can't* intrude unless you do give him permission! We can be sure that the Lord is very angry watching all the injustice going on in this world. The more like Jesus we are, the more angry we are at injustice to innocent people.

And we are also angry at injustice shown to Jesus Himself. He doesn't deserve to be "crucified afresh"! Paul is emphatic: *"be angry!"* Just don't sin at the same time. Don't be a dishrag.

Spectacular corporation embezzlement is the news of almost every day. Even within church organizations it sometimes happens. Africans have sometimes claimed that London was built with wealth stolen from them in colonial days, especially days of slavery. To what extent First World people enjoy their luxury at the expense of Third World people, the most enlightened economist will find it difficult to estimate. But God's angel economists have it all tabulated accurately.

The only safe way to prepare for the final judgment is to count all that we possess as not ours, but only *lent to us* temporarily to be used in trust for those less fortunate than ourselves. If you own a piece of property, don't call it "mine." Abraham did not possess even a foot of real estate, and he is our "father." When Jesus died, He had no money to bequeath. All He had was His robe, which the soldiers gambled for.

"Steal no more"! A good prayer to pray is, Lord, give me the grace from your much more abounding store, to realize that I can claim nothing in this world as really mine. But I do have a Savior!

Ephesians 4:29-32

"Let no corrupt communication proceed out of your mouth, but what is good for necessary edification, that it may impart grace to the hearers. And do not grieve the Holy Spirit of God, by whom you were sealed for the day of redemption. Let all bitterness, wrath, anger, clamor, and evil speaking be put away from you, with all malice. And be kind to one another, tenderhearted, forgiving one another, even as God in Christ also forgave you."

It is more difficult to obey verse 29 if we are constantly engrossed in modern media entertainment, because the "corrupt communication" of modern popular speech becomes ingrained within us, unconsciously.

If we don't want to talk like "Babylon," we must "come out of Babylon" (Rev. 18:1-4). But we can't leave the world, and we are not to become hermits. What can we do?

Paul's counsel would be: resolutely control your radio, TV, DVDs, and CDs. Do not *let* your heart dictate worldliness to you. A prayer that God loves to hear and He loves to answer is the one that asks for a new heart that loves honesty and purity: "Create in me a new heart, O God, and renew a steadfast spirit within me" (Psalm 51:10). Our heavenly Father loves us; He will welcome every one into the New Jerusalem who could possibly be happy there. Life now is simply learning to be happy there.

Every time an impure or filthy expression would escape your lips, check it immediately. Agree with the Holy Spirit that He shall remind you if you forget. Be ready at the slightest moment to respond to His conviction.

Plead with the Lord to enable you to say something always that will be helpful to people. This is number four in those Genesis 12 promises to Abraham (and to you!)—"you shall *be* a blessing."

Paul tells us here that the Holy Spirit is not an idea; He is a Person with feelings just as we have them. He can be grieved and insulted. It takes a rare friend to come back to see you again if you have insulted him in your home. Such a person usually just stays away from now on. The Holy Spirit does, too. (You asked for it!)

The Holy Spirit is a Gentleman. If you insult Him, He doesn't bring down a firebolt on you, He simply walks away. He's the One who "seals" you for eternal life; it's a grievous loss for eternity if you drive Him away from you. Even a church can "grieve" the Holy Spirit; He simply walks away. It becomes like the Temple in Jerusalem after Jesus said, "Your house is left to you desolate" (Matt. 23:38). The architecture and the music are still beautiful, the people are still smiling, and unless you are alive "in Christ" you won't even notice His absence any more than the ancient Jews did up until 70 A.D. when the Temple was finally destroyed.

So, again we come up to that little word that is so meaningful: "LET" all these evil things "be put away from you." "LET this mind be in you which was also in Christ Jesus." "LET him who stole, steal no more." Lay all your sins on the Lamb of God, and LET Him bear them away, for the word "to forgive" in the original means "to bear away" what was evil.

Then Heaven begins here on earth: "Just as God in Christ" forgave you, so now His forgiveness flows out from you to others around you. To be "tender-hearted," ladies and gentlemen, is not to be a "softie;" it's simply the spirit of the King of kings and Lord of lords.

When Does Sexual Love Become Sinful Lust?

 Ephesians 5:1-21

Chapter 9

E PHESUS WAS AS SEXUALLY SINFUL AS WAS CORINTH. The craven lust was all over the Adriatic—the Roman lifestyle. Life was thought good, food was plentiful, the weather was wonderful, the mysteries of sex were intriguing; life was a new Sodom and Gomorrah. "Great is Diana of the Ephesians!" was the popular drinking song.

The similarity to First World life today is striking. The only difference is that our culture today is more dangerously under divine judgment, because ours is *post*-Christian, and those poor people then were yet to discover the beginnings of the faith of Jesus. The judgment that hung over their heads was not what "we" face, with all the light our world has been privileged to see.

Sexual promiscuity lies at the root of an enormous portion of the world's agony, whether in the Third World or the so-called First. It's the basic cause of the AIDS epidemic; it fuels most crime; it flourishes together with violence. Children and teens don't know how to evade its ravages. Even if disease doesn't strike them down, often marriage is poisoned before it begins. Industries are even created by making jokes about illicit sex. The entertainment business that flourishes in Hollywood inevitably gravitates toward sex or violence as its basic appeal for popularity, constantly seeking to infiltrate into children's TV programs and videos.

Whatever word can embrace the opposite of what the biblical word *agape* signifies, it is the modern plague of the human race. The Greek word was *epithumia*, which is translated as "concupiscence" in our English Bibles. The original word meant "a longing for what is forbidden." It's the root idea in that "enmity against God" that we read in Romans 8:7.

Why did God create us male and female? It's this mystery of holy love. But it becomes perverted and is the secret that provides the almost endless energy that fuels this "enmity against God." We would have to coin a word—maybe anti-*agape* would have to be it. It's the impulse to murder God, for "God is *agape*" (1 John 4:8), and that impulse found its satisfaction in the murder of the Son of God at His cross. It still wants to crucify Christ afresh.

Millions of sincere teens of every culture long for some power to clarify the muddle of life and deliver them from this phase of slavery to self, which they instinctively recognize to be slow moral suicide-bombing. They long for pure love; where can they find it?

Ephesians 5:1-4

"Therefore be followers of God as dear children. And walk in love [agape], as Christ also has loved us [with agape] and given Himself for us, an offering and a sacrifice to God for a sweet-smelling aroma. But fornication and all uncleanness or covetousness, let it not even be named among you, as is fitting for saints; neither filthiness, nor foolish talking, nor coarse jesting, which are not fitting, but rather giving of thanks."

It becomes apparent as we move through Ephesians that its key word is *agape*. Never does the apostle command the people to "walk in love" without in close context reminding them of how Jesus has walked in love as He saves them. *Agape* is the very nature of God, but it was never seen so clearly revealed to the universe until the event of the cross. Only in the light of the cross can the mysteries of sex be understood.

That's why Paul is so enthusiastic about this "mystery" now revealed. Even the unfallen angels had no clear concept of the grand dimensions of the character of God until they saw the Father revealed in the Son as One who chose to go down to eternal death rather than see us be lost. At the cross, the character of *agape* is what we contemplate and "comprehend." Then the miracle takes place: our previously anti-*agape* heart is melted, and becomes tender, unselfish, loving!

But now the apostle reveals that his deep concern is this obsession with sex that has so plagued Gentile life. Unless these new converts to Christ understand the horror of this continued sin, they will face dangers like what we see today in AIDS. True, there was no AIDS in Paul's day that we know of, but AIDS is the modern symbol of the terror of "the wrath of God" that Paul warns the Ephesians about.

The "wrath of God" is not like the wrath of man, just as the love (*agape*) of God is not like the self-centered love of man. When God is angry, He leaves you to yourself—the most terrible thing that can happen to you. So with sexual sin; the healing ministry of Christ as "the light of the world" and of "our Great Physician" is constantly at work in our mortal bodies; but God looks upon sexual sin in a special way. He says He "hates divorce, for it covers one's garment with violence" (Mal. 2:16). In other words, there is always murder buried in the violation of the seventh commandment. And God hates murder. This violence poisons life on the earth.

If a person violates that holy commandment, there is often a penalty paid in one's physical organism; the immune system can break down (as it does in AIDS). "The Great Physician" does not want to walk away and leave the person to himself, because if that happens the healing ministry that God has built into our physical system is cancelled. Our Great Physician does not want to walk away! *But, He may be forced to.* That is why sexual diseases are so rampant and deadly.

Thank God, modern medicine can sometimes relieve the misery. But there is the greater pollution of soul that always follows. Multitudes would give anything if they could erase the memory of a few moments' foolish indiscretion. It's in love to us that God has given us His holy law of Ten Commandments, not as "kill-joy" negative commands but as a wall to protect us against destroying ourselves. Everybody needs a "wall" to protect him or her.

When the law of God is understood as a "law of liberty" (James 2:10), the apparently negative commands metamorphose into ten precious promises of eternal joy. *Believe* the preamble that says, "I am the Lord your God who brought you out … of the house of bondage," and the Lord says, I promise, "You will not commit adultery"! Freedom at last from the plague!

Procreation is a solemn gift of a holy God; it's not only "not fitting" to jest about sex, it is perilously close to blasphemy. God doesn't like it, but children and youth pick up whatever crude and irreverent language is popular. They learn to despise and ridicule the holy privilege of procreation. Only those who are privileged to "survey the wondrous cross on which he Prince of glory died" can learn to hate the debauching language that is at heart a hatred of God.

Ephesians 5:5

"For this you know, that no fornicator, unclean person, nor covetous man, who is an idolater, has any inheritance in the kingdom of Christ and God."

We are not to conclude that the sins of fornication (sex between unmarried people) or adultery (the same committed by married people) cannot be forgiven if the sinner comes to the Savior and receives the gift of repentance. For a very good reason, God hates this sin in particular (Mal. 2:14-16), and the Son of God was tortured and murdered because of it—*but He will forgive*. His forgiveness actually takes the sin away, and forever after, the forgiven sinner hates that sin like poison.

But if he does repent, he prays David's prayer of repentance, where the psalmist says he feared he may have lost his soul forever (Psalm 51:11). It's the unrepented sins of fornication and "uncleanness" that must bar the way into the New Jerusalem for the simple reason that people carrying such pollution would be totally miserable there. The reason why no person guilty of sexual sin "has any inheritance" there is not because of some extreme prudishness on the part of our heavenly Father; if anyone enters the New Jerusalem with that sin still buried in the heart, he will become a poisonous cancer eating out the heart of the City. It's love (*agape*) that is forced to close the doors. And it's love to the unrepentant sinner, too, for he would find the purity of eternal life in the Holy City to be a hell to his soul.

"Covetousness" is included. Possibly Paul's intent here is to mention the tenth commandment that says, "You shall not covet your neighbor's wife" (Ex. 20:17). All pornography feeds the violation of that simple command of holiness, because all such lust is impure coveting. Watching another woman's immodesty is the sin of covetousness, the lure of pornography. Paul did not realize what sin is until he discovered the meaning of that command against coveting one's neighbor's wife (Rom. 7:7). Paul was as human as any of us!

Ephesians 5:6, 7
"Let no one deceive you with empty words, for because of these things the wrath of God comes upon the sons of disobedience. Therefore do not be partakers with them."

That blessed gift of forgiveness, worth so much more than Donald Trump's or Bill Gates' billions, can be given free. Believe that the Savior has forgiven you; ponder it; count its blessings; appreciate it and what it means; and you will forgive yourself—something you once thought you could never do. You will become "pure in heart" (Matt. 5:8). "The wrath of God" simply leaves "the sons of disobedience" alone.

Frightful loneliness, that is, away from God!

Ephesians 5:8-14

"For you were once darkness, but now you are light in the Lord. Walk as children of light (for the fruit of the Spirit is in all goodness, righteousness, and truth), proving what is acceptable to the Lord. And have no fellowship with the unfruitful works of darkness, but rather expose them. For it is shameful even to speak of those things which are done by them in secret. But all things that are exposed are made manifest by the light, for whatever makes manifest is light. Therefore He says: 'Awake, you who sleep, arise from the dead, and Christ will give you light.'"

The apostle says something strange here. Instead of saying as usual that we were once "full of darkness" or we are now "full of light," he says we were "darkness" personified, and we are now "light" personified "in the Lord."

What he means is that God's New Covenant promise to Abraham is being fulfilled—we *are* a blessing wherever we go because we are the Light itself shining in us, that is, Christ is dwelling in us by faith. We don't have to worry about giving Bible studies to our neighbors or fellow workers; silently, probably unconsciously, we are exuding light and a knowledge of the gospel by the way we live and speak.

Paul urges the Ephesians again that since they are the "light" personified, "walk as children of light." Again, he is not laying upon them a legalism burden; he is reminding them not to forget *who they have become* through the grace of Christ.

The Holy Spirit is in the process of bearing fruit within them. Having become acquainted with Jesus, they have learned to love "goodness, righteousness, and truth," and their love is contagious.

Other people are saying, "I want what those people have!" That is what the word "evangelism" means.

But conflicts are unavoidable. These people are no longer attending the drinking or sex parties; but the apostle's counsel to "expose them" does not mean necessarily that they are to create stormy sessions of denouncing these things. By not taking part, the "saints" are automatically "exposing" the evil without the necessity of railing against it.

People often say we must "denounce" sin, "tell it like it is!" There are times when "Elijah" is needed; but don't envy that prophet, because more often "Elisha" is needed, the quiet, gentle spirit. In fact, Paul has told us in Ephesians that we are to seek "lowliness and gentleness" (4:1). It may accomplish much more than "Elijah" is able to do.

In fact, Paul expressly warns against trying to "speak of those things which are done by them in secret." The Holy Spirit will flash into their minds the details that only He can bring up safely. He brings the light that "exposes" the evil; let Him do it unless you have unmistakable evidence that it is your duty to do so.

The call to "awake, you who sleep," reminds us of the call of Jesus to His Eleven to "awake" in Gethsemane. Too much is happening today in the church and in the world for any of us to "sleep." Practice good health reform, keep your body healthy and your mind clear and active. "Abstemiousness in diet is rewarded with mental and moral vigor," says some old counsel.

Ephesians 5:15-21

"See then that you walk circumspectly, not as fools but as wise, redeeming the time, because the days are evil. Therefore do not be unwise, but understand what the will of the Lord is. And do not be drunk with wine, in which is dissipation, but be filled with the Spirit, speaking to one another in psalms and hymns and spiritual songs, singing and making melody in your heart to the Lord, giving thanks always for all things

to God the Father in the name of our Lord Jesus Christ, submitting to one another in the fear of God."

It seems unusual to us that Paul would speak of getting drunk with alcohol in the same sentence as he speaks of being "filled with God's [Holy] Spirit." But there may be a connection. Alcoholics Anonymous teach their successful people never to say that they are no longer "alcoholics." The once-captives know that they must forever remain humble, for alcoholism *per se* is never curable, they say.

Whether they are right or wrong, we must never claim that we no longer have a fallen, sinful nature, even though the Lord has given us victories. We are still sinners by nature and will be until glorification. But by the grace of God we condemn sin in our sinful nature—Christ condemned sin in the nature He "took" from us. The alcoholic can condemn within himself the sin of drinking.

Thank God for the "psalms and hymns and spiritual songs" the Holy Spirit has inspired. Don't deprive yourself of the comfort and strength that singing New Covenant songs inspires. But be thoughtful. Don't sing carelessly, any more than pray carelessly. The Father seeks thoughtful people who worship Him in Spirit and in truth (John 4:23).

Generally, we don't learn overnight to "give thanks always for *all* things." If we had more wisdom and understanding, we would do so, for Romans 8:28 says that "all ... work together for good to those ... who are the called according to His purpose" (which is *you*, if you believe and appreciate the message of Ephesians!).

Chapter

10

Is Marriage Still God's Plan for Us?

 Ephesians 5:22-33

O NE OF THE PROBLEMS THAT TROUBLED THOUGHTFUL citizens in the Roman Empire was marriage. Even the darkest-minded pagans realized in their hearts that they didn't want the human race to degenerate to the level of animals, even though they knew that unbridled lust would drive them there. There must be some way that marriage could be made to work, otherwise civilization itself would collapse. Paul appealed to this widespread concern.

Thoughtful people today realize the same. Often sexual attraction draws two people together, they marry; then when the novelty of sex wears off, problems arise, and now we have another unhappy home. Often, two live together and holy marriage is forgotten.

Paul faces the problems head on in Ephesus. One of the most precious fruits of believing the good news of Christ is the transformation that it performs in any human heart regarding love in marriage. That was the solution that the apostle gives for Rome's problem. Remember, his idea of *agape* is tied to his idea of the love that led

Christ to die our second death. Can the quarreling husband and wife understand this theology? Paul believes, Yes. The Spirit of God can impart truth to their understanding.

Ephesians 5:22-24

"Wives, submit to your own husbands, as to the Lord. For the husband is head of the wife, as also Christ is head of the church; and He is the Savior of the body. Therefore, just as the church is subject to Christ, so let the wives be to their own husbands in everything."

By extracting these verses from their setting, some have thought of Paul as a hard-hearted misogynist. They conjure images of a brutal husband demanding slave-master-like authority over frustrated wives, and then claiming that this is the will of God. Satan wants to spread distorted ideas of the character of God, that He is hard and severe. What does Paul mean by "submit"?

Note: he has just said the same thing to *everybody else*, using the same Greek word, "submit." He tells everybody, "submit to one another," in the same way he asks wives to "submit" to their "own husbands in everything." Paul can't be asking everybody to be a doormat!

Neither is he asking any wife to become a doormat to a brutal husband. If he can, Paul wants to help believing women not to get tangled up with men of that character! He is simply asking everybody in the fellowship of the church to be Christlike in getting along with each other. Nothing more; nothing less. "Submitting to one another" even before a word is said; choosing constantly to do to others as we would want them to do to us; recognizing that "one another" may have more good judgment than we have; and depending on the gifts the Lord has given each of us.

If the wife remembers that she needs the Savior, she will remember what she needs to do—that submission to Him is what the husband needs, too! Jesus will keep His promise to send both the Holy

Spirit; the wife will see in her husband the man that God wants him to become, and she will believe in what the Lord wants to do for him. *She will cooperate with what God wants to do for him.* And therein she will find her happiness.

That is how in her submission "to her own husband" she will in truth be submitting "as to the Lord." This gives us a deeper insight into how the church relates to Christ as "the Savior of the body." The husband will protect his wife with his own body; blessed is the wife who realizes the role God intends her husband to fill, and who believes that Christ is the Savior of them both. He will hear her prayers for her husband.

In Ephesians Paul is not discussing what a believing wife should do if her husband is an unbeliever, but in 1 Corinthians 7 he gives practical gospel good news to any wife who has that problem. "The unbelieving husband is sanctified by the [believing] wife, and the unbelieving wife is sanctified by the [believing] husband. ... How do you know, O wife, whether you will save your husband? Or how do you know, O husband, whether you will save your wife?" (vss. 14-16). In other words, don't hinder by unbelief what love (*agape*) may accomplish!

Ephesians 5:25-27

"*Husbands, love* [with agape] *your wives, just as Christ also loved* [with agape] *the church and gave Himself for it, that He might sanctify and cleanse it with the washing of water by the word, that He might present it to Himself a glorious church, not having spot or wrinkle or any such thing, but that it should be holy and without blemish.*"[1]

It may be shocking to us to discover that conjugal, sexual love is also *agape*. No, not lust; this is why Paul is so emphatic that there

---

1. A later edition of the NKJV does not have "it" for the church, but "she" and "her."

should be no jesting about sex; it's a serious, even holy, subject, for it is "procreation," that is, something we share with God. When the husband understands what is the character *of Christ*, he will love his wife with a true love, something far deeper than what we call the "chemical reaction."

For one thing, it's a love that outlasts physical charms (Abraham Lincoln gave Mary Todd a wedding ring in which was inscribed, "Love is eternal"). Someone has written famously that "love is a precious gift which we receive from Jesus." In times now long forgotten, a popular song was titled, "Silver Threads Among the Gold." It told of a love that endures even when hair turns white. The story of Isaac and Rebecca in Genesis 24 illustrates how conjugal love can be true.

+ The Lord "sent His angel" to guide in the choice of Rebecca (vs. 7).

+ The Lord gave "success" in finding her, and His blessing to what was in fact a blind date courtship (vs. 12).

+ The Lord had "appointed" her for Isaac (vs. 14; but that doesn't mean that He wants us to marry someone we can't love! His leading becomes the greatest joy of the one who prays and seeks).

+ The girl was a "virgin" (vs. 26; that made it much easier for the Lord to give the happiness He wanted to give!).

+ Don't rush into marriage (cf. vs. 21).

+ Her parents were consulted; they recognized the leading of the Lord (vs. 50).

+ Isaac and Rebecca enjoyed what is probably the happiest marriage of love recorded in the Bible (vs. 67).

An amazing detail emerges from these verses: Paul's expression "not having spot or wrinkle" is a quotation from the little-read Song of Solomon in the Old Testament (4:7, for example; this confirms the inclusion of this book in the canon of the Bible!). Thus Paul recognized that a happy marriage is a picture of what will be Christ's eventual union of heart with His people who form His church in these last days (cf. Rev. 19:7, 8).

Ephesians 5:28-30

"So husbands ought to love their own wives as their own bodies; he who loves his wife loves himself. For no one ever hated his own flesh, but nourishes and cherishes it, just as the Lord does the church. For we are members of His body, of His flesh, and of His bones."

The use of the subjunctive mood of the verb ("ought to love their own wives") does not mean that this is to be a heavy duty. When temptation comes to a married couple, a thought of the marriage vow is a healthy reminder; but again, victory is more than a legal obligation being fulfilled. What holds a marriage together through thick and thin is the faith that believes, "It was God who brought the two of us together! We must not tamper with His doing!" Then the realization of love can return.

It's the same as when we read that "the Lord brought [Eve] to the man" (Gen. 2:22). It's not superstition that speaks of a marriage as "made in heaven." Every step that leads to marriage is to be characterized by wholesome modesty, so that memories forever after may be happy and pure. It's the memory of God's leading, something more awe-inspiring than mere lust in sex!

A superficial view of what Paul says (taken out of his context) assumes that he is promoting a thoroughly selfish reason for a man to love his wife ("he who loves his wife loves himself"). But Paul's constant emphasis of *agape* assures us that he is constrained by an unselfish love. He is reminding husbands that God has made the two of them one. Being true to the one whom the Lord brought to him is the sure path to his lifelong happiness; and in his happiness hers is intimately involved, and the children's, too.

Ephesians 5:31

"'For this reason a man shall leave his father and mother and be joined to his wife, and the two shall become one flesh.'"

That's not being selfish! When a husband loves her in this way he loves the institution of his marriage, and he loves what God did to the two of them. So in the end, you can say, he loves God too. He simply wants his marriage to bring honor and glory to the One who invented the idea long ago in Eden.

Ephesians 5:32, 33

"This is a great mystery, but I speak concerning Christ and the church. Nevertheless, let each one of you in particular so love his own wife as himself, and let the wife see that she respects her husband."

Why doesn't Paul say that the wife should love her husband with the same *agape*? Is the apostle being fair?

There may be a profound reason here that is part of the good news of the gospel.

Her role is different. She was not created to be the "house-band" that holds the institution together (the word "husband" comes from that idea). "Rebecca" doesn't go looking for "Isaac." It's "his" place to go looking for "her," and "he" loves his role as God has planned it.

Adam was lonely in Paradise, and wanted to search for some kind of Eve; but she didn't try to woo him. Love is the initiative of the man; woman is won by his love for her. The original plan sometimes doesn't get worked out, but thank God it can be respected and blessed nonetheless. But we must note that very seldom if ever do we read in the New Testament that it is *our love for Jesus* that initiates our salvation; *it's His love for us*. Faith is clearly revealed as our heart appreciation of Christ's love *for us*; therefore faith is taught in the Bible as our healthy response to His love for us.

A woman's devotion is the response to what she perceives is the man's love for her. It's far deeper than a mere emotion; if her husband proves himself a man who commands "respect" (vs. 44, KJV, "reverence"), she *will* respect him. If he is a worthy man, at times she may even regard him with a mysterious "awe." Her heart will be forever happy in his love.

How Our Every Battle Can Be Won

Chapter
11

 *Ephesians 6:1-12*

PAUL LOVES THE IMMATURE BELIEVERS IN CHRIST AS HE loves the mature ones. Now he has a message for children.

Children have a problem from birth, as do we all. We all have inherited a sinful nature and our carnal heart by its very nature "is enmity against God; for it is not subject to the law of God, nor indeed can be" (Rom. 8:7). Thus we are not to be surprised that even little children *naturally* have a mind that is in opposition to their parents.

Their relationship to their parents is in miniature a replica of their natural hostile relationship to God which they will consciously understand as they grow up. As little children they need the reconciling ministry of the gospel of the grace of God. It is manifested through the love of the parents, whose message the child "receives" (note that word!) long before he can understand the gospel in words.

Assuming that a child's physical needs are being well met, if it is a sweet and lovable child, that probably means he is already "*receiving* the reconciliation" (see Rom. 5:11). The conflict between the love of self and righteousness has begun already, though in infantile dimensions; the ministry of parental love is already "reconciling" in its nature.

The goodness of the child is not innate goodness—no one has any; in ways suited to the child it is already the gift of salvation "in Christ." Blessed is the parent who understands what is going on; the message of Ephesians is already bearing fruit!

Ephesians 6:1-3

"*Children, obey your parents in the Lord, for this is right. 'Honor your father and mother,' which is the first commandment with promise: 'that it may be well with you and you may live long on the earth.'"* [1]

Let's face the honest truth: some parents are very difficult for *any* child to "honor." Often even the more upright parents are so rigidly legalistic in their supposed righteousness that they are a roadblock to the child's harmonious spiritual development. Still, there is the divine commandment to "obey your parents": it must be obeyed. But how?

Thank God, the Giver Himself of the commandment became a Child, and as such He was "in all points tempted like as we are, yet without [the] sin" of dishonoring *His* parents (cf. Heb. 4:15). But here's a shocking question: as a Child, was Jesus tempted to dishonor His parents? Didn't He have as His mother the most wonderful woman in the world? (One great church says Mary was "immaculately conceived" in the womb of her mother—which the Bible does not teach.)

Mary confessed her need of a Savior, just as we all must confess our need of One (Luke 1:46, 47). She loved her Child Jesus, no question about that; but often a mother can love her child but at the same time be tempted to be exasperated at him/her (and in our experience be more than tempted!). We have a glimpse of Mary's temptability that

---

1. Paul took this not from the familiar "Ten Commandments" of Exodus 20 but from Deuteronomy 5:16.

way in the story of her encounter with her Son in the Temple when He was only 12 (2:43-50).

On the way home from Passover, she frankly forgot about Him during a day's travel. Meanwhile, He was staying behind to witness to the nation's leaders, *the right thing for Him to do.*

Her exasperation with Him is evident in her words, "Son, why have You done this to us?" You can feel the thunder and lightning in her words, "Look, Your father and I have sought You anxiously."

He responded to her honestly, confronting her with the truth, but He did not sin by dishonoring her. She knew well who His true Father was: He said, "Did you not know that I must be about My Father's business?" Yes, children, *know* that Jesus was *tempted* then to dishonor Joseph and Mary! Yes, He was "in all points tempted like as we are, yet without sin." Now, you join Mary in confessing that you need that same Savior to save you from yourself, and to give you grace to honor your parents, no matter how ornery they may *seem* to be.

Children, only by the grace of that Savior can you obey this commandment to "honor your father and your mother," because no one in the world has perfect parents. Your sinful nature you inherited from our father Adam tempts you to disobey this commandment. But through the faith of Jesus *you can* and you *will be* victorious over temptation!

Jesus makes His promise to children: "To him who overcomes I will grant to sit with Me on My throne, even as I overcame and sat down with My Father on His throne" (Rev. 3:20). Yes, there will be children sitting on that "throne"!

Ephesians 6:4

"*And you, fathers, do not provoke your children to wrath, but bring them up in the training and admonition of the Lord.*"

Fathers are busy men, harried by constant pressures for the care of the family. They must provide for the physical needs of the children whom they have brought into the world; but impatience can prompt them to expect too much of the children and "provoke" them into childish sin.

But it's still sin; and in the books of heaven is it not written against the father's name? Father needs that same Savior; and he *has* Him for his Savior already! Now it's time to remember. Let him thank the Savior more earnestly and heartily for His grace. There is precedent in the Bible for fathers taking the sin of their children upon themselves in a corporate sense, illustrating the God-given sense of responsibility that rests upon fathers (see Job 1:5). In these last days especially, the Lord will give special help to needy fathers because of His promise to send us "Elijah the prophet before the coming of the great and dreadful day of the Lord. And he will turn the hearts of the fathers to the children, and the hearts of the children to their fathers" (see Mal. 4:5, 6). Some may call this a psychological ministry, but it is a miracle of divine grace that is so desperately needed now.

Ephesians 6:5-8

"Servants, be obedient to those who are your masters according to the flesh, with fear and trembling, in sincerity of heart, as to Christ; not with eyeservice, as men-pleasers, but as servants of Christ, doing the will of God from the heart, with good will doing service, as to the Lord, and not to men, knowing that whatever good anyone does, he will receive the same from the Lord, whether he is a slave or free."

The original word translated "servants" is *slaves*. This makes Paul's letter to the Ephesians seem astonishing to us. Didn't he know that slavery is morally reprehensible in the sight of God? Why did the apostle of Christ apparently, *on the surface*, appear to support it?

1. Paul being the firebrand that he was, could have stirred up the greatest slave rebellion known in ancient history since the time of Spartacus (71 B.C.). But if he had done so, his fate would have been the same, for God did not send him to free the slaves politically or economically. The most precious gospel that Paul proclaimed gave practical-living *relief* to slaves, lightening their burdens, and making life tolerable for them "in Christ."

2. In a very real sense, Christ came to bring life "more abundantly" to the many slaves of the ancient world (John 10:10). Not only is God concerned for the suffering of multitudes today, He was concerned for those slaves anciently!

3. Paul's brilliant idea of corporate identity was the secret of their finding relief. The idea was simplicity itself, but powerfully effective: they were now to regard themselves not as slaves any longer to their cruel masters *but as slaves to Christ!* Amazing! But that's what Paul says. The apostle has found a secret that poor Spartacus never dreamed of.

If they would believe (have faith in and trust) the truths of this letter to the Ephesians chapter one, they would see themselves in a new light. The great controversy between Christ and Satan was raging in the hearts of their cruel masters, indeed; but as the believing slave welcomed his new identity "in Christ," the fruit was seen in his life. The unbelieving master was affected. Inevitably, he saw himself also in a new light—he couldn't help but have a deep conviction that in being cruel to his Christian slave, *he was in fact treating God that way*, for he saw God revealed in the believing slave. Paul had discovered the best advice ever given to any slaves!

Paul's critics today regard him as a cruel wimp, advising slaves to "be obedient to those who are your masters according to the flesh." Just change "the flesh" to "Christ," and they are in a new world of relative freedom. If we today are willing to be "men-pleasers" in rendering "eye-service" to our employers or superiors in business or even in the church, we are subjecting ourselves to the status of mere "slaves" in God's sight. It is an impossibility to be a "men-pleaser" and to serve Christ at the same time! Paul's letter to the Ephesians is a clarion call to assert our "liberty wherewith Christ has made us free" (Gal. 5:1).

When the slave who has believed Paul's message lies down to rest at night, before he drifts off to sleep he can anticipate the reward his new-found Master Jesus will give him. He has actually served the Lord in his slavery "in the flesh." Tremendous idea, Paul!

Ephesians 6:9

"And you, masters, do the same things to them, giving up threatening, knowing that your own Master also is in heaven, and there is no partiality with Him."

Paul's gospel found lodging in the hearts of slave masters who already had their slaves. The Roman system legitimized it. The news that there was a slave-master who practiced the love (*agape*) of Christ toward his slaves, traveled faster than the Internet could send it now. Paul, thank you! Your message has lifted great burdens from the hearts of many in your ancient world!

Ephesians 6:10-12

"Finally, my brethren, be strong in the Lord, and in the power of His might. Put on the whole armor of God, that you may be able to stand against the wiles of the devil. For we do not wrestle against flesh and blood, but against principalities, against powers, against the rulers of the darkness of this age, against spiritual hosts of wickedness in the heavenly places."

Imagine the courage that this brought to the hearts of the slaves! The little platform of their own private battles of soul has been glorified into a platform in the great cosmic struggle between Christ and Satan. They have now become players in this grand war of the ages; they have been entrusted with a glorious responsibility and destiny. They are now somebodies!

The same Spirit that actuated Christ now actuates them. They sense a close intimacy with Him. A strange new peace now floods their hearts. It's not the "self-esteem" promoted by the mega-church pastors; *it's healthy biblical self-respect.*

In chapter 12 we explore the "whole armor of God" that Paul says we are to "put on."

Chapter 12

Getting Ready for Life's Battles

~~❦~~ *Ephesians 6:13-18* ~~❦~~

THERE ARE TWO BIBLE TEXTS THAT APPEAR ON THE surface to be self-contradictory. One is what Jesus said in Matthew 11:28-30, "My yoke is easy, and My burden is light," versus the other one, the rather stern command of our beloved apostle Paul when he says, "Fight the good fight of faith" in 1 Timothy 6:12.

Jesus and Paul are not at odds, surely; can we conclude therefore that this "good fight" is what Jesus means when He says that His yoke is "easy"?

The Lord's use of His word "easy" needs to be understood and appreciated. The word is not to be denied or disparaged; Jesus said it, He means it. He was wise when He said it, for Satan is constantly trying to convince us that becoming a true Christian is something only a few specially "strong" people can manage to do.

The truth is that there is not one "strong" person in this world; the greatest heroes in the Bible were weak—King David for instance fell flat before a woman's pornographic temptation; Peter folded ignominiously under a mild temptation from a mere girl and denied Jesus cravenly.

Jesus is rightly seeking to encourage ordinary people like you and me to believe that it is possible to follow Him and enjoy companionship with Him—in fellowship of spirit. We understand that Marines who fight together in hard battles become life-long buddies.

Eternal happiness in the kingdom of God will be this never-to-be-forgotten fellowship with the Son of God in fighting battles of faith. You two (Jesus and you) will always have a nodding wink between you that nobody else in the universe will fathom. That "white stone" He gives you in the judgment day has within it a "new name written which no one knows except him that receives it." You keep the secret with Jesus forever (Rev. 2:17). Imagine the whole universe wanting to pry into what you and Jesus keep private between you! And this, all because you made the choice to believe and appreciate what Paul tells us is the privilege of wearing "the whole armor of God" in the battles we face.

Ephesians 6:13

"Therefore take up the whole armor of God, that you may be able to withstand in the evil day, and having done all, to stand."

The King James Version renders it "take unto you," but the New King James Version correctly gives the idea that the armor is something you "take up." It's waiting for you to take it "up." It's lying in your pathway where you can't miss it. It's like the Roman soldier's armor that has been lying by his side all night while he has been snatching a little needed rest, but in the morning that's his first job—to "take it up" and put it on.

Your first job each new morning is to "take up" this blessed "armor." The Roman soldier may at night dream the most delightful dreams of holidays and pleasure, but the morning light reminds him that he must be ready for the stern battle again today.

Paul is very likely writing these words while he is looking out the window watching Roman soldiers on duty. Their job is not only to "stand," but to "withstand," for their very standing attracts the arrows of the enemy to try to force them to fall. So girding on the armor physically includes girding on the determination of soul to win this new battle today.

And the war is being so fiercely fought that if the soldier doesn't make any progress forward that he can see today, if he simply "stands" where he is, that will be a victory! Sometimes standing still is progress. The commander will commend his soldier for simply "having done all" that it was possible to do. Think of our heavenly Commander commending us likewise!

In our spiritual struggle, we are sharing the brunt of the attacks together with our Commander, Jesus; our battlefield is "heavenly places," realms where *spiritual* battles are being fought. No one else, even in our personal family or among our classmates at school, or our fellow workers in the factory or the office, may have an inkling of what struggles we are going through. Never mind, the Commander knows; He has that glint in His eye. He sees you, He understands.

Ephesians 6:14

"Stand therefore, having girded your waist with truth, having put on the breastplate of righteousness,"

The Roman soldier first ties on his leather belt or the equivalent of our bullet-proof vest. There is a covering for his vital organs that must be defended against a sword. Even if he loses a limb he can survive; but he must not lose a heart or other organ.

Truth is a precious entity that doesn't come lightly to anyone. Even little children fight this battle of truth; they are constantly tempted to tell or act lies. It requires as much of their moral fortitude to tell the truth in a playground squabble as for a CEO to tell it in a financial court of law. Blessed is the child who can come to the age of accountability before God with a keenly developed love of truth.

Yes! For example, the child can understand and believe the simple prophecies of Daniel and can reason out with firm conviction who the "little horn" is of chapter 8 and can make his decision that in the final crisis of earth's history he will be true to the Lord God of heaven and to His holy law and His holy Sabbath day. If children can be "girded with truth," can't all of us also?

Jesus said, "You shall know the truth and the truth will make you free" (John 8:32). One of the grandest titles of the Lord Jehovah is, "Lord God of truth" (Psalm 31:5). Jesus said furthermore that He is personally "the way, the truth, and the life" (John 14:6). No one can deny truth in any particular and still be loyal to Jesus!

But truth always involves bearing a cross; that's why Jesus said that He *is* "the truth," because truth always involves the crucifixion of self.

As Paul was watching the Roman soldiers, he thought of "righteousness" as being our "breastplate." The word righteousness does not have a clear connotation for many people, for it sounds "theological." It means simply right judgment, the confession of truth, the choice to be loyal to the basic principle of being straight and upright—all this requires self-sacrifice, or its profession is null and void. Paul encourages us to "stand therefore" defending what is right and letting ourselves be defended by it.

Ephesians 6:15-17

"And having shod your feet with the preparation of the gospel of peace; above all, taking the shield of faith with which you will be able to quench all the fiery darts of the wicked one. And take the helmet of salvation, and the sword of the Spirit, which is the word of God;"

When Jesus commanded us to "go into all the world and preach the gospel to every creature" (Mark 16:15), He meant that we must wear spiritual "shoes." The "shoes" are what make it possible for us to "go."

In the expression "the preparation of the gospel of peace," the word "preparation" implies clearing a highway for the king to come, taking away hindrances or obstacles (Matt. 3:3, for example, "Prepare the way of the Lord," repair the road, the king is coming). Paul's idea is to have good shoes put on properly so there is no obstacle to hinder your mission. And the good news of "peace" will open doors that are presently closed by prejudice.

Jesus knew that we would meet with opposition and suspicion.

As we go to proclaim the last message of salvation, we must let the people know that we are desirous of their best good. Here is where the message of health reform and medical ministry fit in with the proclamation of the gospel. It literally "prepares" the way. The idea of "a preparation of peace" is appropriate.

As Paul studied the armor of the Roman soldier going into battle, he judged the shield to be the indispensable article. Fighting was dangerous business because the enemy shot arrows tipped with fire and poison. The shield must be deftly maneuvered. How does Paul see "faith" as analogous in spiritual warfare to what a shield does in physical combat?

It's nice phraseology, but what does he mean?

The shield is grasped by one arm while the other arm grasps the sword. The two are complementary—one is defensive in battle, the other is on the offensive.

When we are proclaiming truth there is a kind of spiritual adrenalin that nerves us, but when the truth is attacked and we are on the defensive, we are especially tried in faith. Are we sure we are right in our understanding of truth?

New Testament definitions of faith are closely linked with the demonstration of the love of Christ at His cross; faith is a heart-response to that love. But faith also bears within itself the confidence that the cross, despised as it is now, is truth that will triumph. If you are a soldier in a Roman battle, the confidence that your cause will triumph will strengthen your arm which bears your shield. It will be more adept at protecting you from these "fiery darts." Confidence and trust are also elements of Bible faith. To "believe in Jesus" is also to believe in the triumph of His cause.

Ephesians 6:18

"Praying always with all prayer and supplication in the Spirit, being watchful to this end with all perseverance and supplication for all saints—"

The idea is a full-hearted devotion that appears on the surface to be extremism to people whose devotion is only lukewarm.

It is illustrated in Paul's life himself who said: "For to me to live is Christ and to die is gain" (Phil. 1:21). But Paul is not some person unusually created, different from us; he many times confesses himself a sinner by nature just like all of us. What then has made him like he is, totally dedicated to Christ?

The answer: he has seen something we have not seen so clearly. And he has spent his energies writing this letter to the Ephesians to tell us what he sees—how Christ expended Himself in redeeming us.

His equation is simplicity itself: "the love of Christ compels us [constrains, KJV], because we judge thus: that if One died for all, then all died: and that He died for all, that those who live should live no longer for themselves, but for Him who died for them and rose again" (2 Cor. 5:14, 15). What Paul is saying is that we will find it impossible to go on living for self *if we appreciate what it cost the Savior to save us.*

As time goes on, more and more people will sense the motivation of that constraint until a corporate body of saints, 144,000 in mystic number, will "follow the Lamb wherever He goes" (Rev. 14:4). Christ will see His character mirrored in them; they will be to Him what a loving bride is to a husband she respects. The "marriage of the Lamb" will have come; then all we individuals will come *as guests* to the Wedding, while the church as a corporate body will be the Bride. That group will be the "all saints" that Paul speaks of here.

You have your part with them as you are "watchful ... with all perseverance and supplication" for others.

Even the "Good-bye" Is Good News

AS WE COME TO THE END, WE ARE IMPRESSED AGAIN BY the courtesy and kindness that has pervaded Paul's writing. It's love (*agape*) in action. It's what the angels announced over the plains of Bethlehem at the birth of Jesus when they sang, "On earth, peace, good will toward men" (Luke 2:14). Paul lets that same "good will" shine brightly to the last word.

This good-will kind of love pervaded the church in the time of the apostles. It attracted people, and was one reason for the growth of the church in that first generation. It's a joy to read again one of Paul's farewell remarks as they usually come at the close of his "letters." Although this one was very likely intended to go far and wide in winning souls to Christ, it was also originally meant for the one church at Ephesus.

His few personal remarks help us appreciate the warm, outgoing person Paul was. (Well, wait a moment: no, he wasn't *naturally* that kind of a "personality" when he was persecuting the saints! The love of Jesus made him become that way.) If you had been a member of his congregation you would have loved him as a pastor and you would have cried too when he told everybody good-bye for the last time.

Here is where he asks the "saints" in Ephesus to remember him in their prayer:

"Praying always with all prayer and supplication in the Spirit, being watchful to this end with all perseverance and supplication for all the saints—" (Eph. 6:18).

The "battle" for which the "saints" need "the whole armor of God" is framed in prayer. The closer the people of God come to the end of time and the final test of the mark of the beast, the more they will *want* to pray. Facing the "time of trouble" and the close of probation will draw on their souls from deep down as never before in history. They will be keenly aware of how intensely the closing scenes of the great controversy are being played out. Prayer will not be a brief legalistic duty imposed as something one must "do" before getting in bed at night. The little formality "prayers" remembered before opening church meetings will be replaced by earnest heart cries to heaven. Those who are following their High Priest by faith in His closing work of atonement will want to cling to Him closely, their hearts deeply, profoundly moved.

If these final scenes were to be postponed until decades or centuries in the future, we today might not feel that sense of urgency in prayer. Our prayers would hardly be "*all* prayer and *supplication* in the Spirit." Those are serious petitions! But this lack of such earnestness in prayer today has been characteristic in the world church for well over a century. Among those who profess to understand life in the Day of Atonement, public prayer is often as coldly formal as it is among Christians who have no such understanding of truth. Those who feel moved by urgency are often assumed to be "alarmists."

But Paul's plea is not alarmist emotional excitement occasioned by cataclysmic current events. Such media excitement dies out as the crisis fades from public attention. The foundation of serious Holy

Spirit indited prayer is the historicist understanding of the prophecies of Daniel and Revelation. It's the reality of world events leading to the heavenly sanctuary being cleansed that impacts the very core of one's being.

The spiritual condition of the church worldwide is pictured in the parable of the "Ten Virgins," *all* of whom "slept." When the cry went forth suddenly, "The Bridegroom comes!" five sprang awake and trimmed their lamps to go to the "wedding." The other five had carelessly neglected to get oil, and it was too late now; they were shut out.

As we read this parable together with what Revelation says about the "marriage of the Lamb" (19:7, 8), it becomes clear that the five wise "virgins" sleeping is the same lethargy as the Bride-to-be neglecting to "make herself ready for the marriage." The parable does not say that the Bride eventually refused to "make herself ready." But the five foolish virgins did. They refused to "buy" oil when they could.

What Paul says here applied to the "saints" in his time—Christ's ministry in the *first* apartment of the heavenly sanctuary, just after Pentecost.

But now is the *cleansing* of the sanctuary when He ministers in the *second*. It's even more vital to stay close to Him in prayer. Our foe is getting desperate; he still hopes to win the great controversy against Christ. He has only a short time left in which to throw all his resources. Like an army bottled up where there's no way out and it fights wildly, so is Satan today. He knows he was defeated at the sacrifice of Christ on the cross; his desperate ploy is to keep the last days' church lukewarm, sleepy, absorbed in the world, up to the time when it's too late to go "buy" any "oil." He tells his angels, just keep the saints absorbed in their fun and worldly business, and we'll win yet. May this study in Ephesians function as a wake-up call!

Paul's appeal in closing could well have been written for this week's Internet news. The message of Ephesians is complementary to that of Daniel and Revelation—"present truth" (cf. 2 Peter 1:12). The apostle reminds the "saints" to pray for other followers of Jesus, not only for ourselves; we are a "body," and the needs of others rest upon our hearts as well. We are counseled, "Let this mind be in you which was also in Christ Jesus" (Phil. 2:5), and that "mind" of Jesus cares for the needs of "all the saints" (Eph. 3:18).

Ephesians 6:19, 20

"And for me, that utterance may be given to me, that I may open my mouth boldly to make known the mystery of the gospel, for which I am an ambassador in chains, that in it I may speak boldly, as I ought to speak."

Paul knows that he is a chosen messenger for Christ; he knows he has been highly honored by the Lord; the Lord has raised up churches as the fruit of his labors; yet he feels that he needs the prayers of these people so the Lord can bless his preaching and writing! Here's a humble preacher who makes room for the Holy Spirit to work.

The more Christlike a person is, the less worthy he will feel to preach and teach the gospel, and the more he will long for the blessing of the Lord. And sometimes it will be when he feels the most helpless and undone that the Holy Spirit can strengthen him the more. As Paul was coming to preach in Corinth he just about came unglued with fearful tension: "I was with you in weakness, in fear, and in much trembling" (1 Cor. 2:3). His humility revealed the genuineness of his dedication.

"How ready is the man to go whom God hath never sent;
How timorous, diffident, and shy, God's chosen instrument!"

The King James Version sounds a striking warning: "Woe be unto the pastors that destroy and scatter the sheep of My pasture! saith the Lord" (Jer. 23:1). "They prophesied by Baal and caused My people Israel to err. ... For from the prophets of Jerusalem profaneness has gone out into all the land. ... Who has stood in the counsel of the Lord, and has perceived and heard His word? ... I have not sent these prophets, yet they ran" (vss. 13-21). Jesus wants us to labor so faithfully and thoughtfully that our "fruit should remain" (John 15:16). Public acclaim and the records of baptisms may not reflect the true reports recorded by the angels.

No wonder Paul was so moved to ask for the prayers of God's people in Ephesus! To proclaim the gospel effectively anywhere takes more than any person has in him!

Ephesians 6:21-24

"But that you also may know my affairs and how I am doing, Tychicus, a beloved brother and faithful minister in the Lord, will make all things known to you; whom I have sent to you for this very purpose, that you may know our affairs, and that he may comfort your hearts. Peace to the brethren, and love with faith, from God the Father and the Lord Jesus Christ. Grace be with all those who love our Lord Jesus Christ in sincerity. Amen."

A significant detail is almost lost here that we could easily overlook. It's Paul tying together "love (*agape*) with faith."

"Love [*agape*] with faith" (with "peace" and "grace" nearby) is the formula that permeates Paul's messages. To him, "faith" is not defined as a self-centered "trust." We must not misunderstand its true nature.

Paul's idea of faith is not egocentric; it's the mirror-reflection of Christ's *agape*. Faith is aroused in cold human hearts by the revelation of that kind of love. All humans are born empty, devoid of it, having yet to learn it. The gift comes by the preaching of the gospel when *agape* "is poured out in our hearts by the Holy Spirit who was given to us" (Rom. 5:5). Then "faith works by *agape*" and it never fails to produce "fruit" in obedience to all the Ten Commandments of God (cf. Gal. 5:6). It includes that much neglected Sabbath commandment.

Paul's teaching of salvation by faith creates in the human heart a deep love for the Lord's holy Sabbath day that comes as a gift each week. That faith moves mountains of apathy; people wake up. The gift is long overdue, but the Lord says He will give it. Even now there are large numbers beginning to rejoice in a love for the Sabbath. As we near the final issues, that love will deepen as God's people understand and proclaim its truth more fully. The coming of the "mark of the beast" will usher in the revelation of its opposite—"the seal of God" in true Sabbath observance (see Rev. 7:1-4).

———————

With this fresh outburst of saving good news Paul brings his most precious letter to a close. There are some of his readers who will receive "in sincerity" the gift of "grace" that he is passing on from "the Lord Jesus Christ." Their hearts have been deeply stirred, for time and also for eternity, by reading or hearing the message in this letter to the Ephesians.

May you and I be among them!

More Books About God's Heart-Warming
Good News
By the Author of YOU'VE BEEN "ADOPTED"

A New Look at God's Law:
How the Ten Commandments Become Good News

"Wait a minute—God's Ten Command-ments are *Good News?* I've always thought of them as ten severe, nearly impossible prohibitions written by a stern God!" This book turns our thinking upside down about the commandments. Read and believe the Prologue when God says that He "has *already* brought you ... out of the house of bondage," and His Ten Commandments become assurances of blessings. This breath of fresh air will lift loads from your heart!

Paperback, 100 pp.

In Search of the Cross:
Learning to "Glory" In It

Published over and over, and in many languages, *In Search of the Cross* explores the journeys of those who have taken the road to the cross: Jesus, Mary Magdalene, and Paul, and the author's own joyous experience. As we read we too experience the same "journey," and realize that beyond any doubt the cross casts out human fear. A touching and compelling book for our time.

Paperback, 135 pp. [00149]

The Lion That Ran Away:
Children's stories from Africa ... and other places

Can children understand the "message of Christ's righteous-ness"? We believe the answer is, Yes. These forty stories, taken from real life, will illustrate for minds young and old how the gospel "works" in our everyday experiences.

In this beautifully designed book are stories the author has told over the years to children in churches he has served. Stories include, "The Lion That Ran Away!," "Moja Gets Saved" (and other Moja the cat stories), "The Elephant That Needed the Dentist," "The Story About the Proud Baobab Tree," and "The Battle Jesus Won When He Was Only 12."

Parents and grandparents will love to read these stories aloud to their children and grandchildren, and those in charge of telling children's stories in church will find this book to be a wonderful resource. *And children will love them too!*

Large format paperback (9 x 8-1/2 in.), 120 pp.

www.ingramcontent.com/pod-product-compliance
Lightning Source LLC
Chambersburg PA
CBHW030314130626
46549CB00002B/852